Little Astronaut
A Memoir in Essays

Maryann Aita

ELJ Editions, Ltd. is committed to publishing works of quality and integrity. In that spirit, we are proud to offer this work of creative nonfiction to our readers; however, the story, the experiences, and the words are the author's alone. The events are portrayed to the best of Maryann Aita's memory and some names and identifying details have been changed to protect the privacy of the people involved.

ISBN: 978-1-942004-42-4

Library of Congress Control Number: 2022933398

Cover Design by David Wojciechowski
Author Photo by Karna Roa

ELJ Editions, Ltd.
P.O. Box 815
Washingtonville, NY 10992

www.elj-editions.com

For Marzipan

A Note on Truth

Most names in this book have been changed, and some identifying details adjusted to protect people's privacy as much as I can without losing story. Dialogue, dates, and the narrative arc of events in my life may not be precise because I am not a computer. These are pieced together from my memories, which may be different than the memories of my family members. But memory is all we have to build the foundation of ourselves; it is possible for multiple truths to exist at once. I've done my best to capture my emotional truth, which may mean I remember rain on a sunny day. A weather report could prove me wrong, but if I was crying, isn't it still a kind of truth?

Since writing this book, I've learned my sister remembers being diagnosed with anorexia at 13. She also told me she was probably restricting her eating before then. I, however, remember learning about it when I was eight, and she was 15. Memory is deeply fallible. My memory is probably inaccurate. Her memory could be as well. Every time we recall something, even in our own minds, it changes. The facts of memory are not equivalent to truth. I've decided to keep these details as I remember because they are my truth.

Table of Contents

Orbit

It's 5:47 a.m. Marzipan paws at my chin. She's been in the litter box recently.

I cover my face with the blanket. She persists.

Outside it is dark, and visible through the space between the curtains are three stars–maybe two stars and an airplane–glimmering and vigilant.

Stars spend their lifespans fighting against their own destruction. They derive energy from internal nuclear fusions, which push outward against gravity's pull: a stalemate. Eventually, a star's energy is exhausted. Its core turns to iron and the star collapses, leaving a black hole in its absence. White dwarfs–stars the size of earth and mass of our sun–explode and disperse their masses and energy into the universe, leaving almost no trace of their existence.

There are between one and 100 octillion stars in the universe. One octillion has 27 zeros, an incomprehensible number of dangling orbs to represent all the stars we can and cannot see. These octillions of gaseous balls of light spackle the universe in roughly 100 billion clusters, which we call galaxies. Among these is the Milky Way, made up of 400 billion stars. Of those stars, we can see less than 5,000 from any point on Earth. Arrayed within those 5,000 stars are 88 named constellations, excluding the almost infinite permutations of unnamed and undiscovered galactic connect-the-dots. Amid these constellations, a single star commands the orbits of eight planets (and whatever Pluto is these days). On one of these planets live nearly seven billion people, 130 billion mammals, and a quintillion insects performing their respective scientific obligations: birthing new insects, new animals, and new humans to replace them when their energies are exhausted.

If the sun were to explode, causing a supernova, it might leave a black hole in its wake, engulfing Mercury, Venus, Earth, Mars, Jupiter, Saturn, Uranus, Neptune, and Pluto. Even if it devoured the whole of our galaxy, one hundred billion minus one galaxies would remain.

If, however, a star at the end of the universe exploded, leaving no trace of itself, we might never know. Pluto, Neptune, Uranus, Saturn, Jupiter, Mars, Earth and its millions of species, Venus, and Mercury would continue in their orbits. Humans would go on piloting planes, traversing city streets, dreaming of being astronauts, watching *Dancing with the Stars,* examining children's knees for bruises, and burning ants with magnifying glasses, undisturbed among one hundred octillion stars.

Outside it is dark, and visible through the space between the curtains is a single star.

I get up and feed the cat.

Dawn

Every Christmas morning growing up in Montana, my brother Martin would slink his way out of his bedroom to wake me up before the sun had begun to rise. He'd have been up for some time by then, staring at the sea of Christmas presents spilling from our living room to dining room.

Together, we'd sit in our dim and silent living room with our grandfather's unwound grandfather clock quiet behind us. It was stopped at 10:47, like a reminder of the hours we'd have to wait for our family to get up. It was our own calculated agony: the subtle tick-tock of our hearts waiting for joy.

§

In our family of six, there was anywhere from five to seven presents given to each family member. Items varied in size, from the obvious CDs and calendars all the way up to the more ambiguous clothing box or large object covered with towels, but:

1) Assuming an average of six presents (p) per family member (q), and an average of six inches (l) by six inches (w) per present, what is the total square footage of Christmas presents under the family tree? Show your work.

$A = (lw)pq$

6 in. x 6 in. = 36 in.^{2}

$36pq = 36(36) = 1{,}296$ in.^{2}

$1{,}296/144 = 9$ ft.^{2} of pure Christmas joy

Packages wrapped in red and green and gold fought for space around our seven-foot, star-topped Christmas tree. The boxes were like planets with broken orbits: a wild mess of gravity and shimmer. It was beautiful. And it was ours.

Family Gifts ca. 1994-2006

- To: Arthur
  - From Mom & Dad: Socks, a shirt, something cool like a set of pastels, underwear
  - From Andromeda: An amazingly artistic and personal craft she made, like a scrapbook of his first year of life
  - From Martin: Something Mom bought
  - From Maryann: Something costing $2 or less, or a sketchpad I asked Mom to buy
- To: Andromeda
  - From Mom & Dad: A scarf, shoes, quilting supplies, calendar
  - From Arthur: Something clever and funny, like a coffee table book of the worst hairstyles of all time
  - From Martin: Something Mom bought
  - From Maryann: Some piece of pottery I'd painted with a cat face
- To: Martin
  - From Mom & Dad: Socks, underwear, a nice wallet, money to fix his car
  - From Santa: Legos
  - From Arthur: Legos, things making fun of Republicans
  - From Andromeda: Something personalized and handmade, like a scrapbook of his first year or a knitted hat
  - From Maryann: Wall calendar, ceramic owl that cost a dollar
- To: Maryann
  - From Mom & Dad: Clothes, shoes, Barbie clothes, Barbie shoes, CDs, gift cards for clothes
  - From Santa: Barbies, Barbie clothes, Barbie horse, stable for Barbie horse
  - From Arthur: Hairbrushes
  - From Andromeda: Something beautiful and thoughtful and handmade, like a quilt made of cat fabric and embroidered with my name
  - From Martin: Barbies, clothes Mom bought

- To: Mom, or Dad, or Mom and Dad
    - From Arthur: A painting he'd done of my father's grandparents
    - From Andromeda: Handstitched quilts, an IKEA gift card we all pitched in to buy, framed photos
    - From Martin:???
    - From Maryann: Some shitty pottery I painted, a book of poetry I wrote, cat ornaments, a sweatshirt
- To: Family
    - From (We all know it's from Mom): Golf Scrabble, Simpson's chess, Monopoly, Simpsons Clue, Trivial Pursuit, Jenga

Our father followed a farmer's schedule, despite having grown up in suburban New Jersey. He'd be up by 5:30 a.m. each day, an hour I've mostly experienced by not having gone to sleep. Our house woke up with him—the coffee pot growled and spit, the kitchen lights burst on. But on Christmas morning my brother and I would bask in the dark emptiness of our house.

Martin would summon me to the living room before the sun, before our father, before the earth was awake. We'd waddle through the black hallway, failing to stifle our giddiness over what lay in store. Once we made it to the living room without waking our parents, we turned on the side-table lights, sat next to each other on the couch, and gazed at the wonder before us.

While Martin and I entertained ourselves in the living room (*i.e.*, I would scold my brother for tearing the corners of the wrapping paper on his gifts while also asking him to do the same on my present), our parents drank coffee. Our older brother, Arthur, would keep sleeping upstairs while our sister, Andromeda, baked corn muffins.

Andromeda baked often: cookies, brownies, lemon bars. She would sometimes enlist me as her helper, though I never understood why she invested such labor into making cookies and eating none. Baking requires a certain tediousness, the agony of precision: flour measured and flattened, conformed to the shape of a mixing cup. I got to add in the vanilla (after my sister poured the proper amount into the teaspoon). I could also add the chocolate chips (after my sister helped me measure out the right amount). I got all the batter. She did most of the work.

On Christmas mornings, she always made corn muffins. I never helped.

§

Even through my teenage years, our family ate breakfast as a unit each Christmas morning. No matter how hungry we all were, we would wait for Arthur to wake up and eat together. By the time we'd sit down for breakfast, Martin and I had been up for several hours, fueled by our unbearable proximity to a pile of toys we could not open. Once, my mother caved to our demands to wake Arthur up so we could eat (*i.e.,* open presents). It was around 10:00 a.m. and neither my brother nor I had gone mad from hunger, anxiety, or a combination of the two. But our mother probably anticipated we were moments from deteriorating into a two-pronged tantrum. So, she trudged upstairs to wake the dragon.

Arthur slumped his way down the stairs, like a groggy bear crawling out of his hibernation den and sat at the dining room table in his usual seat, next to me. My own seat location allowed a perfect view of the Christmas Mountain in the living room while I slathered my corn muffins in butter and jelly. The densely packed, dry cornmeal shapes were unrecognizable after meeting my jam-wielding knife. Sugar functioned as an appeasement in my household. My parents made me eat breakfast with them each day, even throughout high school, but it was more of an assurance that I was awake and ready to go to school on time than a bonding activity. We'd divide the paper among ourselves and eat in reserved silence with the abandoned newsprint of the sports section on the table beside us. That breakfast was usually a chocolate muffin, chocolate éclair, coffee cake, cheese danish, or something equally unwholesome. I've always had an incurable sweet tooth. It was the reason Martin and I were so eager to tear apart our gifts: gluttony.

"I need socks. Where are they?" Arthur asked across the table.

"I don't know. I think they're over there," my mother gestured toward the left side of the heap of presents. "Just go look."

Arthur explored the mound and grabbed a small package in red wrapping paper. He peeled back a corned then ripped it open. He put on a pair of new socks and returned to his post at the table.

Halfway through my corn muffin, my mother saw the agony on my face. She gave in and told me I could open a present. But the magic evaporated when the token present opening ended. The excitement we craved was in the variegated silence of our living room. Martin and I, two fledgling masochists, stared at presents knowing we wouldn't be able to open them for hours. But we sat. Still. So as not to upset our ticking hearts. Not to upset the anticipation of joy. It was our ritual of loneliness, like two aimless astronauts looking for light, and hoping we could will the world awake.

Vanishing Star

This is what haunts me: at twenty-four my sister stood five feet, one-inch tall and weighed only sixty pounds. I recall the numbers without hesitation, as if I were reciting my own address. I think of my sister mostly in pieces—ages, images, facts: Andromeda, is seven years older than me. She used to dance ballet. I once thought her cheeks looked as though they'd been hollowed out with a melon baller. She earned her GED when she was 16. By then her veins, blue against translucent skin, protruded from her childlike wrists. She liked ice skating when we were kids. She was hospitalized five times that I remember. These glimpses are what lurk deepest in my memories. To make sense of them, I gravitated to numbers, keeping a tabulation of trauma:

	15	the age my sister was when diagnosed with anorexia nervosa
	8	the age I was when my sister was diagnosed
	2	the number of teddy bears my mother purchased for me in hospital gift shops
	3	times my sister was forced into an addiction treatment center
	9	years that my sister, and my family, lived with an eating disorder
+	24	the age my sister was when she crossed the threshold into recovery

But there is no sum total for my sister's illness. Anorexia is rooted in numbers—calories eaten weight lost, inches shed—but it requires a complex language I did not have as a child. Numbers became my armor, a minor defense against pain that squeezed its way to the forefront of my childhood recollections. Numbers are simply how I know where the story begins.

In the summer of 1997, I was about to start third grade, and my teenage sister was a ballerina. One night, our mother and father sat down with her at our kitchen table, while I played with a chipped brown plastic cup on the floor. For some reason, no one made me leave the kitchen (or told me not to sit on the floor). My dad stood and leaned over the back of his chair while my sister and mother sat across from each other.

After avoiding the issue for twenty minutes, Mom and Dad mentioned that Andromeda's dance teacher had expressed concern about her weight, an opinion our parents seemed to agree with.

"We notice you eat a lot of salads, Andromeda," Dad said.

For my entire life, I have retained that single detail from their conversation, as if it were beyond comprehension that eating enough salad could be a bad thing.

There was much more to the conversation of course—ballet, baggy clothes, perfectionism—but it must have seemed less intriguing to me than the inscrutable salad comment. I also remember a picture that had sparked their concern. It was from a couple of months earlier; in it, a teenage Andromeda and Arthur were standing in a hotel room on a trip to Seattle with our dad. Dad placed it on the table in front of her. She looked "thin."

Exhibit A: Inordinate vegetable consumption. Exhibit B: Photographic evidence. Eventually, the word *anorexia* snaked its way into the conversation.

In all my eight years, I had never heard the word. I had no idea what they were talking about, which was probably why my parents never made me leave the kitchen.

At first, I was convinced my sister's disorder was entirely fictional. It sounded more like a character from a book than a disorder. Anorexia, Princess of Galitraxis. It was new vocabulary; it was exciting. In my mind, I began constructing my own definitions.

> ANOREXIA \ an-*uh*-**rek**-see-*uh* \
> *noun*
> 1. possibly a kind of herb
> 2. maybe the name of some ancient ruins.

In 1998, psychologist Peggy Claude-Pierre published *The Secret Language of Eating Disorders*, a book about helping her two daughters recover from their successive battles with *anorexia nervosa*. One year prior, my parents confronted their fifteen-year-old daughter about the eating disorder they suspected she had. Claude-Pierre, and her book, appeared twice on *20/20*, then on *Oprah*. Meanwhile my mother read and re-read her copy of Peggy's book—Mom decided she was on a first-name basis with the woman—as if she were trying to physically absorb its contents. She scoured its pages four or five times that first year, and never picked it up again. Yet Peggy's book remained on a shelf in our house until I left for college ten years later. I wish I had even skimmed its pages, but I was afraid of what I wouldn't find inside it. That book was supposed to have a cure, but Mom never found one in its pages. Why would I?

In 1993, before she published the book, Peggy founded an inpatient treatment center in Canada with an astronomical success rate: the Montreux Clinic. Though she still only accepts the most severe cases—those who have been in and out of treatment and tossed between doctors with no help—Peggy has a 90 percent rate of curing eating disorders without recidivism. Though effective, Peggy's methods are not easily employable in a family with four children. Her practices demand constant attention, encouragement, and flexibility from caregivers, which is not only exhausting, but would have been impractical in a household with a son in college, a teenage boy and girl, and a third grader. Unsurprisingly, my parents were unsuccessful in their efforts to recreate the results on their own.

After their kitchen table confrontation, Mom and Dad took Andromeda to see a new psychiatrist in town. Her name was Dr. Green. "Green like salad!" I said to my mom when my parents mentioned her.

My comment went ignored.

§

After Dr. Green's official diagnosis, my parents' natural response was to place Andromeda in a treatment facility. They could not afford Montreux and, at that point, anyway, my sister would have never been accepted. There was only one center, The Rimrock Foundation, that even treated eating-disorder patients in my home state of Montana. Most of its patients were alcoholics and drug addicts, but it accepted patients like my sister, struggling with anorexia.

My family made a two-hour drive with Andromeda in the new minivan to support her as we pushed her into an addiction center that loosely treated a disorder she didn't believe she had. Rimrock treated anorexia and bulimia as a dependency, like narcotics or alcohol. Andromeda never had so much as a sip of alcohol before her treatment, but she seemed to split her time there between AA meetings and card games.

After my family returned home from checking her in, her counselor called to tell us that Andromeda had eaten chicken strips and fries for lunch. My parents were not as happy about this as I was.

"Well, that's not a surprise," Dad said, unmoved by my sister's sudden reformation.

Not a surprise? I thought. "Isn't that a good thing?" I asked. I had ordered chicken strips in every restaurant for my entire life.

My mother answered my father, still ignoring me: "Of course she did. She's manipulating them!"

It became a tagline for my sister: The Manipulator. My parents and Andromeda had read Peggy's book and talked to a psychiatrist and learned terms like *manipulate* and *anorexia nervosa*, terms I didn't understand. When I think of how often my parents used the word manipulate, I feel naïve for having taken so long to learn the definition.

"*Why is that bad?*" I asked.

My mother doubted Andromeda's sudden progress. "It's not bad. Chicken strips are good, but…she doesn't want to be there, so she's trying to get out faster."

I accepted this answer, though their logic about the chicken strips was still unclear to me. Everything was unclear to me. Instead of rummaging through shelves for our battered dictionary, I continued making my own definitions of words.

> MANIPULATE \ m*uh*-**nip**-y*ew*-leyt \
> *verb*
> to use chicken strips for evil

A week into her treatment, all five of Andromeda's immediate family members visited her, but the minivan dwindled after the first one or two visits. Andromeda was probably in Rimrock for a month, but because my relationship with my big sister was culled from playing Barbies whenever we wanted to once-weekly visits in a hospital, it felt much longer. When I last visited my sister, only my mother and I went. I liked the long car rides with my mom. She was so serious then, straining to hold fragments of herself together in front of her children. The last time she took me, she missed an exit on the highway and had to double back. She checked the clock and failed to keep from swearing in front of me. There was only a two-hour window in which visitors were allowed, and we were in danger of losing at least thirty minutes of it. My mom tapped her fingers on the steering wheel as if it made the car go faster. I told her that it was okay; we had plenty of time. As frantic as she was, I was elated to be there. I didn't mind spending an extra half hour in the car with her.

When we got to Rimrock, the three of us ate lunch and played new card games my sister learned. At some point, my mom gave me the deck of cards to play solitaire and told me to go get more Jell-O from the cafeteria; then she and my sister would talk about things I wasn't supposed to hear. I didn't mind. I liked the cafeteria. Cafeterias meant choices. I could have as many desserts as I wanted, including eight helpings of Jell-O, which we never had at home. I loved those moments alone in the cafeteria. I got Jell-O. And it was all for me.

After a couple of visits with me tagging along, Mom thought it was best that she went alone.

§

Growing up, Andromeda had shown me how to do almost everything the "right" way: how to tie my shoes and how to bake, how to color and wrap gifts, how to find the words in word searches, how to ice skate.

When I was in kindergarten, Andromeda would take me ice skating in the winter evenings. A few minutes' walk from our backyard was South Side Park, an expansive field of green iced over for skating. She would help me lace up my double-blade skates and hold my hand as she glided onto the ice, and I tottered behind her. When I would fall, she pulled me back up and led me around the rink once more, guiding me out of my fear and past my failure.

That first time she was in treatment, brief as it was, stands out in my memory as well as any childhood game or ice-skating excursion. Perhaps because it seemed so out of context. When my sister was released from Rimrock the first time, I was thrilled to see her again. She was frail, but stable. The sight of her was enough to give me hope. After a few days back, her life became a schedule: every action, every meal, every thought was planned. It seemed the only way to manage her obsession with control was by regimenting her life.

My misunderstanding of her disorder grew into a mystified admiration for Andromeda and her ability to restrain herself. I wanted to be her, from coloring inside the lines to counting calories. There was something in her I envied: she was my opposite. She did everything perfectly.

PERFECT \ **pur** -fect \
adjective
like an older sister

Most of the things she taught me—how to fold wrapping paper over the corners of a box, how to measure vanilla extract—are now rote. She had carved her life into a rigid order, and I swooned at its artistry. Slowly, though, the order she etched—her three snacks a day, a crossword puzzle every morning—consumed her.

But she taught me how to do so many things. I thought I was supposed to be like her.

Growing up next to my sister's flat, feminine body, a body she had sculpted with unrelenting discipline, I felt grotesque. My sister went through life backwards: shrinking instead of growing, perfecting instead of mistaking, dying instead of living. She reduced her ballerina silhouette down to a specter of herself. She was the ideal for which women have strived for centuries. I, on the other hand, hit puberty before I was twelve. My breasts ballooned to an absurd size, my body started to jiggle when I ran down the stairs, and clothes clung to parts of me that I didn't know I had. Andromeda was almost nineteen when I was in seventh grade, but people began to confuse her for my younger sibling on the infrequent occasions we were together. Four years after her diagnosis, my sister moved to a town more than an hour from home. My family thought she might get better there, free from Mom, but we saw each other even more rarely than we did during her hospitalizations, and Andromeda continued to shrivel away.

Unlike me, Andromeda had control of her body. Whereas my boobs were of questionable proportions for a middle schooler, hers shrank. While so many girls desired bigger breasts, some telling me how "lucky" I was to be so curvaceous, I wanted nothing to do with mine. Even my mom, whose intentions were well meaning, made me ashamed of them every time I tried on clothing. She would tell me how "flattering this cut is" and how well it "hides" or "distracts" from my neckline. Despite one daughter starving herself, my mother would still make occasional comments about my weight. I remember her once telling me I looked a little plump. I almost walked away crying.

Andromeda was thin. I wasn't. I thought that was what bothered me. But what bothered me was that despite her best efforts to disappear, my sister remained the star of our family. When I was ten, I was already sick of family and friends asking me, "How's your sister?" I wanted them to ask about me. But my childhood was out of order; it was mired with guilt, responsibility, and misunderstanding. I wanted an eating disorder, a mental illness, a magical power—anything special about me, anything to be wrong with me. Instead, I was the stable one, a healthy child in a family steeped in illness: the boring daughter whose parents didn't have to worry about her.

It wasn't until I was in college and Andromeda was in her mid-twenties, that I realized how much like her I'd always been. I wasn't anorexic, but she and I were after the same thing: an impossible, indefinable standard. We differed, though, in where that desire led us. I was left chasing perfection—trying to get the best grades, imposing my own rules, avoiding pleasure, putting all my effort toward college applications, homework, knowledge—but I had no idea what "perfect" even meant. Rather than try to reign over every moment of her life, Andromeda chose to control one thing: food. She agonized over each calorie, willing her body not to eat. She found one aspect of her life over which she could rule absolutely. I realized all too late it was the anorexia that fascinated me, not my sister. It had a hold on her and quickly took the rest of my family in its grasp. Anorexia is a highly visible disease, yet my family almost never spoke about it— and still doesn't. My sister walked around like a ghost, and we treated our shared psychosis with Prozac and as much physical distance between ourselves as we could make. Both of my brothers moved out of state while I was in high school. I counted the days until I could apply to colleges and escape. It took me years to understand that Andromeda was not her eating disorder, but until she recovered, it was hard to see anything else.

As a kid, I wanted to know everything about anorexia and everything about my sister. Like anyone haunted, I wanted to exorcise my ghosts, which meant knowing them first. Being a part of my sister's life, however, was like trying to infiltrate my neighbor's "No Girls Allowed" tree house. I collected incomplete facts about her situation from conversations I overheard between my mother and other relatives or from clues around the house. On our refrigerator, for instance, she and Mom kept a daily meal plan (written on a cutesy Mary Engelbreit notepad with cartoon animals) that included breakfast, which they would eat together; a midmorning snack, which they would eat together; lunch, which they would eat together; an afternoon snack, which they would eat together; dinner, which the family ate together; and an evening snack, which they would eat together. The concept of planning snacks made little sense to me.

SNACK \ **snak** \
noun
regimented one-on-one quality time with Mom

There was food in our kitchen I was not allowed to eat—Boosts, low-fat yogurt, burgers made of vegetables. My sister kept dozens of PowerBars stacked in even rows at the bottom of a cabinet, organized by flavor, that I had to ask permission to eat. Things in my house were not mine; they were my sister's. When you are eight years old and you watch your mom eat six meals a day with your sister, but you aren't allowed to drink what appears to be a milkshake in a can, you start to assume it's your fault.

Andromeda seemed in control of everything. Eventually I found out my mother would tell her if I had eaten any of her food. For my sister, this served to account for any disturbance in her perfectly ordered life. To me, it was an act of oppression.

The last time I ever asked for a PowerBar, when I was nine, my mother said, "It's probably not a good idea. They're really for Andromeda. Only have one if you really want it."

I didn't really want it—every flavor tasted like grass—but I really didn't want to have to ask permission to eat gross food.

"That's okay," I said.

Later that day, I changed my mind. I took my mother's earlier statement as a loose permission to take one—not entirely sure it was all right but figuring no one would notice. I stole one chocolate PowerBar. It was my treasure, forbidden and wrapped in gold. I gnawed through it and disposed of the shiny wrapper evidence. While I was playing by myself in the dining room a few hours later, a doorway apart from the kitchen, I heard Andromeda, her voice shaking, ask our mom why she was missing a PowerBar.

How did she notice? I wondered. My heart sped up.

I'd been caught.

"I know Maryann didn't have one today," Mom said. "I'm sure it just looks off."

It seemed my mother had been reporting my PowerBar dalliances. It became clear I had ruined my sister's perfect order, all because I wanted to be able to choose what I could eat whenever I wanted to eat it. Yes, a part of me wanted to take something of hers, but I hadn't realized how it would upset her, how it would disrupt the balance of things. She could eat anything she wanted, whenever she wanted, and all I took was a PowerBar. One PowerBar. It seemed so small.

Crouched there, digging through wrappers, searching for the evidence, my sister frightened me. She thought she'd mistaken the number of energy bars in her store and she felt helpless. I realized how fragile she was, like a porcelain figurine that I had dropped and made shatter on the floor. Frail as she was, she had a power over me. I was afraid of breaking her. I never told her that I was the culprit, that she wasn't wrong.

And I never willingly took another thing from her.

CONTROL \ k*uh*n-**trohl** \

verb

1. to use pity to inspire fear in others, especially children

noun

2. a sense of superiority over inanimate objects, often by outsmarting them with one's ability to count

Before my sister moved away in 2001, for a job in Helena, my parents were frantic to control her. All while she manipulated them, pretending to follow her meal plans and reporting more calories than she had eaten. The three of them began to act like the scribbles on my coloring book pages, trying to appear put together, but bursting outside the lines meant to contain them.

Andromeda had started antidepressants when she was diagnosed, and she went on anti-anxiety meds soon after, and our mom upped her dose of Effexor somewhere in between. Our dad tried things like hiding one percent milk in the skim bottle, a plan that ended with a bottle of milk poured on the kitchen floor in the center of a triangle of screaming. Mom ate every meal and every snack with Andromeda and gained almost thirty pounds in the first few years. My sister lost weight. Dad told Andromeda she looked like a Holocaust survivor. He wasn't wrong, but our father was, at times, tactless. Our mother was erratic. My sister couldn't admit she was anorexic. It was like they were trying to build a square with only three sides, each miscalculating his or her contribution. There was no way they could add up.

Eventually, Andromeda moved to Helena, a town an hour and a half away. Our parents thought living on her own might be good for her, away from the constant monitoring. Instead, Andromeda became drastically worse, and we ignored it. A long drive made for infrequent visits, and we all chose not to look past the long sleeves, pants in the summer, and Andromeda's word things were "fine." My mother, father, me, and even my brothers were exhausted.

Though some eating-disorder patients—between 30 and 40 percent— fully "recover," the extent of their recovery is up for question. They may be physically healthy, but their emotional security could be unstable. Between 5 and 10 percent of eating-disorder patients die within ten years, the highest mortality rate of any mental illness. Statistically, Andromeda should have been one of the latter. She was only 59 percent of a stable body weight. She weighed sixty pounds when she was twenty-four; I weighed more in fifth grade. It wasn't supposed to be possible to live like that. I'm not one to believe in miracles, but if I ever witnessed one, it was my sister's life.

MIRACLE \ **mir**-*uh*-k*uh*l \

noun
when the math works out even when you miscalculate along the way

Nearly ten years after her diagnosis, my twenty-four-year-old sister, who was as close to literal skin and bone as seemed humanly possible, acknowledged her eating disorder for the first time. One Thanksgiving Day, she sat on our couch and pushed the words out through her almost translucent, tear-stained face.

"I am anorexic."

It was also the first she ever spoke of getting treatment. Close to a decade into a mental illness that had ravaged her mind and body, Andromeda said she'd found a facility she'd be willing to go to: Peggy Claude-Pierre's Montreux Clinic in Canada. She was nervous to bring it up because of the cost but thought our parents might be willing to help. Apart from the expense and the distance, it required that each patient have a caretaker to watch her every day for the duration of the treatment.

"They would need to be there for a year and stay with me 24/7. And, when I thought about it," she hesitated, "the first person I thought of was Maryann."

I swallowed. Hard.

My parents used logic to relieve me of the responsibility. It was an absurd idea, especially given that our mother had no job and no longer had young children to look after. But they both rescued me from having to answer. What I'd wanted to say—what I'd always wanted to say—was *Fuck you for thinking I'll put my life on hold to save you. I can't save you. And I won't try.*

"Your sister can't do it, Andromeda," Mom said, "She has school."

"And she'll only be seventeen," Dad said.

The sentiment was overwhelming; I was not the candidate for such responsibility. At the time, I was in my junior year of high school. I'd recently achieved the coveted milestone of learning how to do laundry by myself. Not only was I unfit to look after another person, but I could hardly look at my sister without tears welling behind my eyes.

Andromeda had plans, too, thinking I could go to college in Canada while she went through treatment, or that I could take a year off before going to school. My sister's world revolved so closely around me that she believed I would pause my life for her.

As much as I wanted to rescue her, I couldn't.

Montreux was not going to happen. We might have been able to come up with the money, but I couldn't stay with her, and my mother had to stay with me. In part, it was my fault she couldn't go.

Instead, Andromeda returned to her life as it was.

Until she lost her job.

§

In April 2006, I had just turned seventeen and Andromeda had driven down to visit my parents and me (our brothers had moved out by then). When I hugged her, my hands nearly wrapped back around myself. My teenage arms rivaled her thighs.

My adult sister weighed 60 pounds then. We learned the exact number later. I didn't believe it was possible to be so small; she was a skeleton I feared would shatter. I tried to ignore the fact that her child-sized pants were slipping off her hips. But she wore short sleeves that day; trying to divert my gaze from her withered arms only left me looking at her face. All I could do was trace the sharp contours of her jaw line and examine her cavernous cheeks, trying to find some remnant of joy in her face. She rarely smiled. She didn't laugh. She hardly spoke, and when she did, she seemed to wander, lost in her own thoughts. It physically hurt to look at her. Her eyes were dimmer than I remembered. They glossed over as she told us she'd lost her job.

One tear slid down her cheek, a lone droplet of emotion that came to rest at the corner of her mouth. Then she wiped it away.

"Angie said…I couldn't…concentrate anymore—and I wasn't," she sniffled, "focusing… on the work," Andromeda explained, each syllable lagging farther behind the next.

Angie, my sister's boss, had known about her eating disorder; it was hardly surreptitious by that point. Because she dearly loved my sister, Angie made every accommodation she could. In the few months before that April, Angie had noticed her fading away, too mentally and physically adrift to perform her job at an embroidery company. Eventually, she had to let Andromeda go. Unknowingly her action became the catalyst to Andromeda's recovery. My parents sat down with my sister and talked for hours about having her move back in with us. I listened, seated on my bedroom floor, tracing the rim of an empty drinking glass. It was going to be constant monitoring, snack schedules on the fridge, and unpleasant dinners all over again. We had reached the point where the only option left was to start back at the beginning.

A few tearful hours later, she hesitantly agreed to stay.

My parents took her car keys. They planned to go to her apartment the next day to get her things. Early that morning, however, I heard my sister across the hall rummaging through her bag. When I woke up, she was gone. As I suspected, she had taken the spare keys she brought with her; I can only assume she had them because she knew what to expect. Of course, if anyone was to always carry a set of spare keys, it would be my sister. Sometimes I wonder if I should have gotten out of bed and said something to her, maybe asked her not to leave. I'm not sure it would have mattered, but I've asked myself why I didn't try: had I given up, or did I feel sorry for her?

My parents spent the next three days calling Andromeda, our psychiatrist, Andromeda's boss, and state mental health services. My sister holed up in her apartment like an outlaw. They were certain needed to be in a hospital or she would have died.

Over the next few days, my parents had my sister legally committed to a general hospital—rather than a psychiatric facility—because she needed (and was unwilling to get) immediate medical attention. Initially, the County Attorney didn't consider her mentally incompetent, but her psychiatrist Dr. Green wrote a letter explaining that my sister's physical state caused her mental duress and that she was incapable of making decisions. When the police came to Andromeda's door, she followed without question. One officer told my parents he was amazed. He hadn't needed to handcuff her, but he wouldn't have been able to anyway: the cuffs would have slipped over her hands.

§

Once she gained some insubstantial amount of weight in the hospital, Andromeda was taken to Rimrock. This time, she was the only eating-disorder patient in the facility. She stayed for a few weeks while our parents contemplated what to do next. A volunteer they met at Rimrock, who had recovered from bulimia a few years earlier, recommended Rogers Memorial Hospital. It was in a tiny, unpronounceable town in Wisconsin a two-day drive from home, but it had both a medical facility and a treatment program. It treated men and women—

one of the few centers in the country that did at the time—and it cost more than a college education.

Anorexia exists in a neglected crevice reserved for deadly diseases with no cure that most people don't consider deadly diseases—insurance companies above all. At the time, most health insurance companies would only cover the cost of getting an eating-disorder patient beyond a "stable physical condition." Based on my sister's multiple hospitalizations, this seems to mean a patient can leave after three to five days of monitored food intake and no weight loss. Our health insurance didn't provide adequate mental health coverage for our family, or for most people in need of mental health care. But my sister's former boss, Angie, let her keep, and paid for, Andromeda's health insurance after she was fired, which meant she was covered for the duration of her three-month treatment. There is no value I could assign my sister's life, but in providing treatment, Rogers inherently appraised it at upwards of $100,000. My parents, like most people, were in no position to take on six figures of debt to save their daughter's life, but it was the kind of decision with only one choice.

In what may be the only documented instance of an insurance company's compassion, my sister's insurance made extraordinary accommodations for her because her condition was so severe. They agreed to cover almost the entire cost. We were lucky. Incredibly lucky.

To stabilize her, she was put in the Rogers hospital wing.

"She had to eat her way out of that room," my mom told me, years later. As I listened, I conjured the image of Hansel and Gretel chewing their way out of the Witch's gingerbread house. Even years after the fact, I couldn't accept my sister in a hospital bed.

"She recovered through fear. The police, the hospitals…she lived like a prisoner," my mother paused, I think with a tinge of regret, and said, "She had to leave the door open when she went to the bathroom."

FEAR \ **feer** \
noun
an effective last resort

Slowly, my sister began eating regularly and as her caloric intake increased so did her mental clarity. Once she reached a point where her body was no longer starving, she could reason again.

She made it through the initial treatment program faster than predicted, and the staff at Rogers wanted to put her into the next phase, which required living on her own in a small apartment for a month. It also required my mother to live in a small apartment next door. In Wisconsin.

My parents were skeptical of her miraculous improvement. My sister had not lost her title of "The Manipulator." None of us had forgotten the chicken strips, the eating regimens she claimed to follow, the "I'm doing well" calls. Debating the next step of her treatment, though, was not something either of my parents wanted to spend more time doing. Mom agreed and went to live with Andromeda for a month, three states away. By that time, my brothers were each rooted thousands of miles from Montana, leaving Dad and me alone for the month of September—the first of my senior year in high school. My father and I shared a two-story house, like a pair of cats existing in the same space, bothering each other only for food and very loud noises.

Neither one of us had seen Andromeda since that April; we'd had only phone calls. We talked to my mother and her often, though. I could hear the smile in my mother's voice. There was an overwhelming sense of relief in our house. It was the calm of the aftermath of a hurricane: damaged, but with the worst behind us.

What I remember most, though, was getting to use my sister's car while she was in treatment. I had always planned to go out of state for college, and my parents didn't think it made sense to buy me a car for two years. I instead got to use my mother's minivan when she didn't need it. My sister's hail-dented Ford Taurus was the highlight of her absence that spring and summer. Perhaps it was the stereotypical apathy of "senioritis," or maybe it was exhaustion from years of guilt but having that car to myself almost made things OK.

At the end of September, the day my sister was scheduled to come home, I stayed at school late to stave off the inevitable disappointment of whatever waited for me at home. If she was going to be the same as when she left, I would have returned to immeasurable disappointment and grief. And if she was going to be different, what would that mean? My relationship with my sister had always been fragmented. She was more image to me than human in the last few years of her eating disorder: skin stretched taut around muscle and bone; spindly fingers like Jack Skellington; veins like rope constraining her.

Part of me questioned whether I wanted her to be well. Even the direst status quo can bring more comfort than an uncertain future. I was used to living with a ghost. What would be demanded of me in this new human relationship? Preternatural communication is very one-sided.

When I finally came home, I waited outside the front door before I opened it, trying to quench my anxiety and act as though my sister had merely returned from a weeklong vacation. As I walked inside, I saw her face, chubby-cheeked and beaming. Her face was flush, and she had a smile I hadn't seen in a decade.

The instant was drenched in ambivalence. Joy, tinged with despondence. It was unfinished and imperfect. It was a beginning. Of what, I didn't know. I took a deep breath, leaving my bags at the door, and walked forward to embrace my sister.

> RELIEF \ ri-**leef** \
> *noun*
> as we hugged, my arms didn't wrap back around myself

Satellites

My cat sleeps during most of the time I spend with her. I envy the ease with which her bright green eyes flutter. Her belly paunch sloshes around as she twists onto her back. And, with two legs sticking upward like signals in the airspace above my bed, her grey chest falls into patterned breaths as she gives in to the luxury of slumber.

Sometimes, she will wake without warning and launch herself onto the windowsill. She will chirp at birds or hiss at the stray cats that meander through our yard—a world she has never stepped into, but knows she owns anyway. Later, she will return to napping.

It is a talent I've never possessed—the ability to exist comfortably in silence. I wish I could wrap my tail around myself and make my body a perfect grey circle. I wish I could fall peacefully asleep. Often, when I am alone in the middle of the night, I am overwhelmed by the urge to rearrange myself. I find myself in the center of my room, spinning, observing. The room I have lived in, organized that way for months, will feel out of alignment. Sometimes, a single piece of furniture is askew and needs to be knocked back into the proper orbit. Sometimes, everything must change. The bed must slide to the opposite wall; the dresser must be dragged diagonally across the floor; my shoe shelf must occupy a different nook.

I'll push the bed from one side of the room to the other. Marzipan, hiding underneath, will slink along the hardwood and follow it to settle again in her shield of darkness. But it won't be quite right there either. I will slide it a few inches to the left, aligning it next to the heater so it sits flush against the wall, the border of our universe. Marzipan will be disturbed again, uncertain why her world has been upended, even though I have performed this ritual dozens of times.

One of my favorite picture books in kindergarten was *Goodbye House*. It was a story about an anthropomorphic bear that said goodbye to every room in his home before climbing into the moving van outside. I had not lived through such displacement then, but it felt deeply relevant to my girlhood self.

My family remained in my childhood home until I was 13. We moved to a smaller house in a newly constructed subdivision before I started eighth grade. I said goodbye to every room before I left for school that morning. In the afternoon, my mother drove me to our new home. My boxes of Beanie Babies, clothing, and computer were waiting in my bedroom, transported there by movers during the day. It was early May and there'd been a blizzard that morning. A constellation of snowflakes welcomed me home.

My new bedroom was upstairs—a promotion. I ditched my full-size bed for my brother's old twin, but the drawers and cabinets underneath it made it an upgrade. The biggest improvement was the entire wall my parents had dedicated to my closet. The eggshell walls, however, made me ache for the peach ones I so loathed during my childhood. Absent of any memorabilia of teenager-dom, the walls felt somehow endless and finite. With only a small window, which was mostly obstructed by the gable above our garage, the room begged for a personality. It was the stifling realm of being a pre-teen, its inhabitant trying to emerge from inside, one tedious chip at a time.

I had stayed up far past my bedtime one night playing on the computer, building a simulated tourist attraction in Zoo Tycoon. While I was busy erecting a fence around some zoo-goers—so I could put a lion in the "exhibit" with them—a text bubble popped up on screen purporting to be one of my zookeepers. She told me the panther exhibit was overcrowded. I sold one of the panthers to a mysterious cyber wildlife preserve. By then, the human/lion experiment had become a cloud of comic book expletives. When the puff dissipated, only the lion remained, roaring in a tiny cage. A few minutes later, the same zookeeper told me the panthers wanted more friends.

What they needed was more space.

I looked over to my unmade bed. My desire for sleep drifted somewhere beyond the eggshell walls. I ignited: the bed *needed* to be moved. But an un-athletic thirteen-year-old girl couldn't lift the wooden monster. She could, however, push it.

Relying entirely on what I credit to be my solid spatial reasoning skills, I orchestrated a path—à la a thirty-seven-point turn—and pushed and pulled the thing, inch by inch, across the beige carpet. I pushed it against the only other open wall in my room, assuming it would fit without obstructing the door.

It did.

I changed something.

I moved the desk next.

Once I discovered this ability, this agency over the tiny universe of my bedroom, it became more frequent. It seemed there was always a more economic configuration for my furniture. Months would pass and, in the night, I'd peer outside, craning my neck to see a star, and be struck by the desire to reconfigure my molecules. I'd spin the world around me in painstaking seconds, pushing furniture across the room until I was out of breath, until my arms buckled, until I was exhausted—too exhausted to push the bed the rest of the way and I would collapse into it, there, in the center of my room. Floating. Asleep. Without an orbit.

For a few months, I would be settled. Then—

The shuffling of a wooden dresser, the sliding of a bed across the floor.

The need to reconfigure has continued, every few months, through four New York City apartments. Like an imaginary friend I've never let go of, this urge has prodded me for more than a decade.

Home alone on Saturday nights, as I am most Saturday nights—not sure if I am there by choice or by default—I ache. My bones and blood vessels fill with the marrow of loneliness and adrenaline of aloneness. My body, so intensely at odds with itself, is homeostatic. It is streamlined by the stalemate of my battling selves: the lonely and the alone.

In those moments, I am grateful to exist in my own space, physically alone save for the silent creature I have adopted. Marzipan will hiss at the cats wandering through our Brooklyn backyard. She is overcrowded.

Yet, I am lonely. My only companion, no longer interested in demonstrating her superiority as a cat living in the same sphere as people, curls into a perfect grey circle and sleeps.

I move. I rearrange my outer universe, struggling, inch by inch, until I am exhausted. I fall into bed with Marzipan, one person and one cat somehow occupying the space of three adult humans on a full-size bed. She sleeps, next to—or on top of—me, her tiny belly rising and falling in a relaxed rhythm, unmoved by the changing universe around her.

Porn Star

I was raised by pornography. My father owned a video rental store for nearly 25 years and raised four children with that single income. My existence depended on movies. Clothes I owned, food I ate was the result of film rentals, including porn. Especially porn. Buried in the catalog of foreign films and action movies was a red curtained room where the lascivious of Bozeman, Montana could rent pornographic films along with the latest rom-com. My father was a smart businessman. In the '90s, he was paying almost double the national minimum wage and provided his employees health insurance. He only had to lay off one of his ten staff in the economic downturn of 2008 and could sell his brick-and-mortar business in 2014, well into an age dominated by online streaming. Pornography didn't make it that far, though. It was the first to go. Why rent porn from a living, breathing person when you can get anything you want on the Internet? But the red curtain remained until after I left for college.

My parents never spoke openly with us about the room in the back corner. It garnered more than one op-ed in the local paper declaring it a sin. Yet, we handed out coupons for free kids' movie rentals on Halloween when we ran out of candy. My oldest brother worked at the store for a few years after he turned 18. He once caught someone trying to masturbate in there, the velvet den of iniquity just a few shelves away from the Disney classics. Mostly, the curtained room at the back of the store was like so much else in my family: a mesmerizing secret, my own Pandora's box.

On my 18th birthday, my friends and I made a list of the world of opportunity that had opened to me. It was brief: smoking, lottery, and porn. I bought a cigar and a scratch-off lottery ticket, but my father's store was the only place we knew of to rent adult films. By then, we also had the internet, an abyss of porn I never began to search. I never once peered behind the curtain, either. My parents didn't acknowledge the porn. They simply said nothing. In absence, I manifested shame.

There were several framed and signed posters of female porn stars on my dad's office walls. He went to porn conventions and met porn stars as if a tedious chore. A quiet necessity. The poster behind his desk was a blonde woman with enormous breasts wearing only red suspenders placed strategically over her nipples and some sexy tighty-whiteys. She may have also been wearing a fireman's helmet. People had scrawled their names all over her boobs and stomach. It felt like something I wasn't supposed to be exposed to as a child. But like the red curtain, no one ever mentioned it, as if ignoring something makes it disappear. *Pay no attention to the man behind the curtain.* Perhaps the hidden nipples shifted it just to the right of appropriate. Next to the poster, on the cabinet behind his desk was our family photo and my school picture.

My father had a printer and DSL before we had them at home, so I did some school projects in his office. When I was 11, I got my first period while typing a paper about Canada for sixth-grade history, Miss Porn Star USA behind me like my Guardian Period Angel. I didn't notice until I was home. Like the anonymous lecher behind the curtain, I, too, masturbated, but did not know the word for what I was doing. I noticed something on my fingers, and upon investigation, thought I had pooped my pants. I threw the underwear away, tossing extra garbage on top of them, and slunk back to my bedroom, ashamed I hadn't noticed earlier. It took me a few minutes, but I remembered a film we watched the year before where they split the boys and girls into different classrooms. Someone had used the word "period," and all the girls in class seemed to know what this meant except me. If not for the movie, I'm not sure I would have known what to do. I ran and got my mother, seeking answers for so much unknown.

§

Most of what I know about my father can be contained in a matter of pages. He was born in New York City in 1953 and grew up in New Jersey, the son of first- and second-generation Italians. He dropped out of college three weeks into his freshman year. He never registered for the draft. He had an affinity for math and played stickball as a kid. His father upholstered furniture and he was the third youngest of four: two boys, two girls. He rode a motorcycle and smoked two packs a day until one day when he stopped smoking altogether. He did LSD on St. Patrick's Day. He got a perfect score on a pilot's license test. He took business classes at night and started his own record store in Ridgewood, New Jersey at age 21. He met my mother at the Marshmallow in New York City, where they danced to "Let's Spend the Night Together" by the Rolling Stones.

Her coat was stolen. He leant her his. They married two years later and are still married forty years later.

My father is quiet and calm, a misfit among the eccentric. More than anything, my father was *there*. Like the porn room was there. A quiet necessity. Something I knew there was more to and never got. He made sure we were housed and clothed. And we were. We existed. But we were ravenous for more.

I hungered for storytelling, for love, for empathy. Movies were constantly, readily available for my viewing and I constantly, readily ingested them. I was a nerdy, lonely, and anxious girl with unlimited access to film and parents who were simply *there*.

When I was a toddler, I requested Kevin Costner's *Robin Hood: Prince of Thieves* every day and my parents let me watch it. Every. Day. Apparently, I was vehement: *Prince of Thieves.* not *Men in Tights,* I'd clarify. As a teenager, I watched, horrified at the degree of violence my mother allowed me to endure as a toddler.

"Mom, why did you let me watch that!?"

"Do you remember any of it?"

"Well, not really. But I feel like I understand the jokes in *Robin Hood: Men in Tights* a lot better."

"Well, there you go," she said.

I may have forgotten the details since, but there is a murder within the first ten minutes of the movie. I cycled through violent action scenes and sex like a View Master, ingesting daily darkness in search of something. Maybe I wasn't in search of anything. Maybe I just needed the noise.

My sister went through a similar phase as a little kid, but her tastes were more refined than mine. She watched *The Wizard of Oz* every day. After dozens of viewings, my dad asked her what the scarecrow wanted. She said she didn't know.

My father could explain budgets and math, but he never taught my sister what the scarecrow wanted. There were so many things we never knew, so many things left to our own scouring of film, our own detective work. So much in our family left unsaid. So much our father, our translator, left us to infer. *Pay no attention to the man behind the curtain.*

§

When I was in fifth grade, we got a *Never Been Kissed* screener and I watched the VHS until the tape was ragged. I've probably watched it more than one hundred times since. It's a romantic comedy starring Drew Barrymore as Josie Gellar, a 25-year-old journalist who goes undercover as a high-school senior and ends up falling in love with a teacher, Mr. Colson. Josie, we learn, was frumpy and ambitious in high school. It's her first real reporting assignment, and a second chance at high school, so she's especially eager to succeed. And to have her first "real kiss." Even at 11, I seemed to understand this woman was my future: a passionate love affair with grammar and a loveless existence. But in the movie, she gets a happy ending, and that's all I wanted.

I never really grew out of the rom-com phase. I devoured them like the gummy bears and popcorn I ate as I watched. I never stopped loving Disney princesses. There was comfort in fairy-tale endings tied neatly into bows. As I got older, I fell in love with John Cusack over and over again, with his boyish charm and manly sarcasm. I followed Drew Barrymore from good to bad, *Ever After* to *Fever Pitch*. I loved Audrey Hepburn and Julia Roberts. I loved Gregory Peck and Hugh Grant. Sure, I'd dabble in thrillers and indie darlings, too. I wanted story, I wanted structure, I wanted *knowing*.

I rewatched films to will my reality into orbit. How could I have had my first period with only a porn star to witness? How could I have so many stories to slide out of a box and into a machine, but so few of my own? How did we exist in such silence?

§

Daddy was my first word. My infant body crawled and mewled down our carpeted stairs, my mother beside me, and as my father walked by, I said "Daddy!" He stopped to pick me up. As the youngest of four children, I felt a special bond to him I like to imagine none of my siblings had. I was the only one of his four children to pick his "name" as the first thing I ever said. Arthur's first word was *light,* Martin attempted to say *goat,* though he only got past the first syllable, and Andromeda made up her own word, a name for her blanket, and we counted it.

Realistically, my first word was probably babbling. It may have even been a default choice, spewing the name of the parent I could pronounce over the one sitting next to me. An *m* sound is much harder to make than something like *d*. My first word was likely a matter of motor skills. We are allowed to assign as much importance to our own life events as we want, and I'd like to think it's more significant than that. But sometimes I wonder if I'm trying too hard to make a happy ending.

The Geography of Flight

Archaeology: A-

When I was eight, my mother, father, three older siblings, and I took a family portrait and hung it above the piano in our dining room. The piano belonged to my father's father, but none of us could play it, nor did my parents see investing in lessons as worthwhile. Eventually, we sold the piano, but the photo remained there, an artifact of our proximity. In it, my mother and father sit next to each other, surrounded by their four children. My sister sits next to my mother and one brother stands between them. My other brother—the oldest and tallest sibling—stands behind our father. I am in the lower right corner, my hands grasping my dad's forearm. I am missing a tooth.

A decade would pass before the six of us took another photo together.

Introduction to Cartography: A

In my childhood home, my oldest brother Arthur, who was ten years my senior, lived upstairs, the sleeping giant at the top of his beanstalk. His bedroom was carpeted in green and distinguished by a hole in the plaster wall from where he had punched it once. In his turret, he designed video games that would swear for him, played Dungeons and Dragons in the middle of the night, and woke up in the afternoon.

His lair doubled as an art studio; canvasses, brushes, and oil pastels speckled the dark green floor. Palettes arranged in rainbows laid open on his desk, begging to be stroked by a child's hands—but I was not allowed beyond the threshold.

He was my "big big" brother, whom I admired for his advanced motor skills, his ability to play chess, and the fact that he was in college—a place I'd wanted to go since I was seven and learned what it was. But my brother and I lived in two time zones within the same house, our existences split by the decade between us.

My sister inhabited the other upstairs bedroom. Andromeda's unpunctured pink walls were interrupted only by a shelf with a twirling ballerina encased in glass. It rained glitter when you shook it.

She never shook it. And wouldn't let me.

Andromeda made her bed with hospital corners, but down the stairs, to the left, alone at the end of the hallway, my bed exploded with stuffed rabbits, teddy bears with missing eyeballs or limbs, and clothing items that had defected from my dresser or Barbie's. It wasn't unusual for the comforter to have migrated to the carpet.

As I accumulated toys and papers and clothes, they found their way to my bedroom floor—landmines along my path from sleep to breakfast. Andromeda seemed not to own things; her floors were immaculate and foreboding.

A row of stenciled teapots and roses served as a cheap crown molding to the peach walls of my own bedroom. My mother had orchestrated their design and painted each teapot to look like Mrs. Potts—to match my *Beauty and the Beast* bedspread. As much as I loved the teapots (probably subconsciously aware of the labor my mother put into this demonstration of affection for her daughter), I hated the peach walls.

I hated the peach walls because they were boring.

I hated the peach walls because they existed before me.

I hated the peach walls because they were not the light pink walls my sister had.

Although, I was glad they were not the booger repositories of my brother Martin's room, anchored between my bedroom and the bathroom. A few feet down the hall from my own toy storage facility, you could find Martin's tubs of Legos and tiny plastic body parts nestled in the blue carpet. When Martin eventually vacated his room—to take over Arthur's lair—I commandeered it to build a Lincoln Log village for my Barbies and Beanie Babies. The plastic stars on the ceiling that glowed in makeshift constellations made their home authentic. Sometimes, my brother and I would lay on the floor, pretending to stargaze, despite being one flight of stairs from the yard and expansive Montana sky.

Our yard was divided by a concrete walkway. On one side, lush grass and an ancient elm tree. On the other, an enormous pine tree blocked the sun, leaving only dirt below it. This was the side of the yard that we kept our picnic table on, a fact I didn't question until adulthood. Under the picnic table, with only dirt beneath us, Martin and I would conduct illicit activities.

My mother liked candles, so she used to buy those sliding matchboxes in the not-even-an-arsonist-would-need-this-many-matches size. Martin, my closest brother in age at five years my senior, liked to light them. When my mother caught on to this, she began to hide the matchbox in the back of the highest cabinet. Our parents needed to stand on a chair to reach it, but Martin could recruit his wiry elementary-school sister for counter-climbing expeditions to retrieve the matchbox. I always accepted these missions.

With matches in hand, we would slink our way to the backyard: matchstick bandits on the run from fun-killing parents. We always sat under the pine tree. Around us, dry pine needles blanketed the ground, except for the patch underneath the withered wooden picnic table. This is where we lit matches.

Martin would slide open the box and strike one, holding it between his fingers as the flame turned from blue to orange and back as it crawled down the matchstick. This is how we would entertain ourselves on days when the upstairs rooms were empty. Martin wouldn't drop the match into the dirt until it burned to almost nothing. Sometimes, he would burn himself and light another. The explosion of flame always surprised me. Each burst of fire left as suddenly as it came. My brother liked to kill the flames, and I liked to watch them disappear.

U.S. History: A

Our family's version of Risk was unplayable because it had been thrown around the room so many times most of the army markers were missing. Still, we kept it in the attic as though it held some historical significance to our family. It was a relic of our legacy as sore losers. And even sorer winners. The game simulated more than the tactics of war—ethics tend to abscond during strategy board games, just as they do in times of battle.

To prevent the United States from collapsing during the Civil War, the Union's strategy was to leave half of the country destitute. Union General William Tecumseh Sherman made a nearly 300-mile march through Georgia in the winter of 1864, stealing food, killing livestock, and burning the houses of southern civilians who resisted his army of 60,000. Confederate forces pushed ahead of them, running south, destroying bridges and food stores to impede the Union troops. Sherman divided his soldiers and they marched, in parallel, thirty miles apart, lugging potatoes and grains, butchering cows and chickens, and decimating the Georgian landscape.

In 1865, Sherman's soldiers applied this scorched earth policy as they burned their way through South Carolina. With few supplies and even lower morale, the Confederacy surrendered that April, preserving the geographical and legal borders of the United States. The post-Civil War South then entered what is known in history textbooks as *Reconstruction*. From the Confederacy's perspective, Sherman's scorched earth left surrender as the only option. In Sherman's view, his "March to the Sea" was self-preservation through self-obliteration.

When cornered in a game of Risk, my brother Arthur would usually respond by instituting an "alien attack," or simply uprooting the game board. Every subsequent reset would lack some fallen plastic soldiers, until there were no longer enough pieces to play.

Drama 101: A+
Who Won't Eat Their Dinner Tonight?
Episode 2

    INT. KITCHEN – EVENING, 1998

    Meatballs move around a plate of spaghetti…

                    MARYANN (VO.)
                Our   family   ate
                dinner   together
                every   night
                while   I   was
                growing up.

    …noodles spin around a fork like hair
    around a curling iron…

the forkful of pasta moves to a mouth, spots of marinara sauce abandoned at the corners of it.

> WOMAN (O.S.)
> Andromeda, are you *sure* you don't want any spaghetti?

ARTHUR, 19, glasses, short brown hair, a bandage on his left shoulder, eats the forkful of pasta.

ON ARTHUR'S RIGHT, SITS MARYANN, 9, long messy brown hair. She has a fork in her mouth and stares at her brother.

> WOMAN (O.S.)
> Andromeda?

> ANDROMEDA (O.S.)
> (whining, tinged with anger)
> Nooo, Mom.

From Maryann's POV, we watch ARTHUR push food around his plate.

MARTIN, curly hair, 13, eats in silence next to DAD, salt-and-pepper hair, Italian nose. He wipes his mouth with a napkin.

On Dad's left, MOM, the family matriarch, twitches as she speaks.

```
                      MOM
               All right.
```

Her reddish-brown curls bounce around her
head. She scarfs a meatball.
Maryann examines the bandage on her oldest
brother's shoulder.

Forks and spoons clatter against silence.

```
                 MOM (CONT'D)
           Arthur had an operation
                    today.
```

Pre-algebra: A-

My brother was 19 when he was diagnosed with Hodgkin's Lymphoma in 1998.

Years earlier, my sister had been diagnosed with *anorexia nervosa,* which she would fight until she was 24.

Nine out of ten patients with Hodgkin's Lymphoma fully recover—one of the most curable types of cancer.

Approximately ten percent of eating disorder patients die within ten years—the highest mortality rate of any mental illness.

Problem: If your oldest brother has a 10% chance of dying in the next five years and your sister has a 10% chance of dying in the next decade, what are the odds at least one of them will die before you see your 19th birthday? Show your work.

Answer: (10% + 10%) x (Your teenage brother losing his hair + your older sister's clothes don't fit your ten-year-old body) = watching two of your siblings starve, depleted of all drive to fight for survival.

Introduction to Anthropology: A+

At eighteen, I left Bozeman, Montana to go to college in the hyper-inflated heart of New York City. Both of my brothers, my sister, my mother, and father came with me to New York—one of the few times our family has been together in the last decade. I bid my three siblings goodbye with a pat on the back and held my mother while she cried. My father was the last to say goodbye and the farewell I most clearly remember. On an East Village sidewalk outside a diner that would cease to exist within a year—which would become a bakery that would cease to exist, which would become a sushi place that likely no longer exists—we embraced in the unfamiliar swelter of an east coast summer.

I have never liked goodbyes. I don't know how to give them. Perhaps because I always find hugs last too long. I don't like hugs—the touching, the invasion of personal space, the unnatural pushing together of bodies in some effort to show affection, to leave a part of yourself with another human being—but hugs seem to be a convention of farewells. I think this is something my father and I understand about each other.

"I'll miss you," he said.

"I'll miss you, too." As I hugged him, I remember wanting it to last longer.

It would be four months before I next saw my parents. The length of our separations expanded each year after that. In my three years at NYU, I returned home three times, the last the summer of 2009, before I graduated and made my roots in New York City permanent. Seemingly within days of my commencement, Mom and Dad sold their house in Montana and embedded their own, child-free roots in Florence, Arizona—a city whose population may be equally divided between prison inmates and retirees.

My brothers had both permanently left Montana years before our mother and father. Arthur, the oldest, moved out at eighteen, then back in to undergo chemo, then to Ohio, Tallahassee, back to Bozeman for his final remission CT scan, until he settled in Philadelphia with his wife and their collection of unicorns. Martin, who moved in and out of our house with the same consistency of a cat secretly living off two families, eventually made his permanent home in California. Despite being the least responsible of the four of us, he was first to get married—to a woman with a young son. Andromeda fled our hometown for the Montana state capital—an hour-and-a-half's drive from Bozeman, through fields of cattle, bison, llamas, and horses—when I was in eighth grade. She was the last to leave the state. A couple of years after our parents left, Andromeda packed up for Portland, Oregon. After having a baby, she and her husband moved to Arizona to be closer to Mom and Dad. I remained in New York City, living in three boroughs in five years. In that time, I spent a total of 16 days with my parents.

Journalism: A
Like Father, Like Pie

Aaaay," says an Italian man—with more grey hairs than black—to the butcher. His daughter says she thinks he sounds like Fonzie.

"Can I get three rib-eyes?" He asks and the butcher grabs some steaks to weigh.

He purchased a winter home in Florence, Arizona in 2007, when Maryann, his youngest child, graduated high school. When she finished college in 2010, he and his wife made the move permanent and sold their house in Bozeman, Montana.

Maryann hasn't spent much time with her parents since then but is visiting for Thanksgiving on the first vacation she's had in several years.

"I haven't had more than a few hurried moments alone with them outside of an Embassy Suites continental breakfast in the last six years," says Maryann, who is waiting with her father in the familiar gleam of grocery store lighting in an Arizona Safeway.

"There wasn't a lot of time between the collective fury of my siblings' weddings," she continues. "My brother got married in August 2010, my other brother in 2012, and my sister in 2014. Their anniversaries are all five days apart."

Dad turns to his daughter and asks if she is excited for steaks.

"I know they're your favorite," he says. Quietly, his 26-year-old daughter replies, "Yeah."
Dad puts his hand on Maryann's shoulder and sighs. The physical resemblance between them is minimal, stopping at their Mediterranean skin tones and brown eyes.

"You know," says father to daughter, "I'm sorry. Sometimes I forget how much younger you are than everyone. You went off to New York and you were the only one who never moved back. I feel like we should have done more. We are really proud of you."

Maryann's eyes avert to the pumpkin pie in their shopping cart. Earlier, Dad had let her buy an entire pie, knowing she would be the only one to eat it.
A small smile peeks out from Maryann's face—the family resemblance is stronger now.

"Thanks, Dad," she says.

Breaking the comfort of silence that hangs between father and daughter, the butcher returns.

"Here ya go!" he says.

"Can I get you anything else?" Dad looks to his daughter and pats her on the back.

"You want anything else?" he asks.

Maryann simply shakes her head. Δ

AP Biology: A-

Hodgkin's Lymphoma is one of the most curable types of cancer despite it affecting the blood and lymphatic system, which transports white blood cells around the body. Arthur had lumps on his lymph nodes removed through surgery, underwent chemotherapy and a bone marrow transplant, among numerous scans, tests, and medical procedures ranging from inconvenient to inconceivable. It was difficult for me to reconcile how *curable* could be so complicated. For a disease with such a great outcome, multiple surgeries, regular IV drips, and laser beam blasters (at least, that's how I always imagined it) seemed excessive. My mother and I suspect the numerous medical complications he later dealt with in his twenties and thirties originated in his chemo treatments.

As with most cancers, the cure for lymphoma most often includes surgery and a combination of chemotherapy and radiation. Arthur didn't need radiation, but both treatments fight the disease by attacking the body's cells without regard to whether they are cancerous.

Cancer treatment is akin to emptying a machine gun in the enemy's general direction: there's a high risk of friendly fire. Because of this lack of specificity, treating Lymphoma is likely to destroy white or red blood cells along with cancerous ones. Healthy body cells are supposed to be able to repair themselves, but, either way, cancer forces a person to wage war against their own body.

Drama 102: A+
Who Won't Eat Their Dinner Tonight?
Episode 87

```
INT. Kitchen - 1999
An unembellished chicken cutlet and pile
of lettuce on a plate.

Pull    away    to    reveal    ANDROMEDA,
approximately 16, dark curly hair.
```

                    ANDROMEDA
          No, I don't *want*
          a hamburger.

DAD, at the head of the table, slams his
fist.

THE FAMILY startles. We see mother, father,
two sons, two daughters around the table.

                      DAD
            Just eat, Andromeda!

Dad grabs a hamburger and throws it on
Andromeda's plate. He slams a fork down
next to her

MOM, Dad, and Andromeda yell at each other.

MARYANN, 9, cries. She picks up the corded
phone on the wall behind her and calls her
friends who live down the block.

                    MARYANN
          Hi, Sarah. Can I—
          Can I come over? I—
          Umm...
                (she listens)
          OK. Thanks.

We follow Maryann to her bedroom. It
explodes with stuffed animals. She gets a
backpack and fills it with toys.

We continue to follow her out the back door.

     MOM (O.S.)
Maryann! Maryann! Where are you going? Come back. Dad's sorry.

     MARYANN (V.O.)
It was the only time I remember my father yelling at any of us. He and my mother would argue, but the dinner table showdown was the only ostentatious display of emotion I ever saw from my otherwise logical and tranquil father. Even more surprising, though, was how ready I was to begin running.

Geography: A-

My sister would often ask to take me with her on road trips around Montana. She'd always attend my speech and debate meets in Helena, where she lived, and once wanted me to stay overnight with her after a meet. (Helena was an hour and half drive.) This required I get a permission slip signed so I could be released to her.

"Do you want to stay with her?" My mother asked when I explained my sister's request.

"I'd rather spend two hours on the bus with my friends," I said, "but I don't know how to say that to her."

"Me neither."

My mother signed the slip and my speech coaches released me to my sister, waiting on a residential street, looking like a little kid wearing her mother's clothes. My friends asked why I was leaving to which I rolled my eyes and muttered "my sister." As I walked off the bus, my coach/sophomore English teacher must have perceived the dread I could not completely mask because he asked me if I wanted to go. I sighed and shook my head gently.

"But she's here now," I said.

"Cheer up," he said.

My peers rode the bus the two hours back to Bozeman, singing and laughing and sleeping all the way, my battalion forging ahead without me.

The following summer, Andromeda drove with me up to Kalispell—a six-hour car ride—to stay with her for three days at a craft festival where she was selling her quilts. We bonded through misanthropism. We made fun of a band of out-of-step cloggers in mom jeans (the men and women). We critiqued the other artists' work at the craft show, awarding mostly positive reviews except for the man who made wire sculptures of horses—they looked like coat hangers reshaped into ovals with legs and a neck. The artist was the only member of the craft fair interested in trading artwork with my sister. We teased him like schoolgirls behind his back, despite neither of us having any sculpting skills to speak of.

One morning, I caught a glimpse of her leg as she changed in our motel room. Her thigh was the circumference of my chubby bicep. It looked like someone had stretched her skin over the muscle, like saran wrap encasing her sinews and musculature. At the time, my twenty-one-year-old sister probably weighed between 70 and 80 pounds. At 15, I was 130.

I couldn't believe she was standing. I thought she'd have a heart attack there and I'd be trapped in northern Montana, with no cell phone and no driver's license: no means of escape.

College-prep Math: B+

Problem: Montana is the fourth largest state in the union in terms of land mass and the 44th in terms of population. You could drive for seven hours—with no traffic—and either still be in Montana or have made it to Canada. You have $300, no passport, and no car. How do you leave?

Answer: Report cards.

Philosophy: A+

Before I left for NYU, Martin took me out to get a cup of coffee because I wasn't old enough to go out for a beer.

"So why are you going to New York?" he asked.

"Because I want to get away from here. Experience something different, I guess."

My brother paused for a while and sipped from the giant coffee mug in front of him.

"It doesn't matter where you go. Everywhere is the same. People are the same," he said.

"They may be the same kind of people, but they'll be new people."

"True, but you'll find that it's still the same."

I didn't drink coffee then, so I mulled my answer over the frothy chai in front of me.

"Well," I said, "I'd like to find that out on my own."

"That's a good point."

Martin moved to California that summer.

Music: C-

My father used to sing along to the Frank Sinatra tunes he pumped through the speakers in our house while he prepared dinner each night. While my brothers, sister, and I all still lived at home, my parents made a point to eat together every night. We only relaxed this ritual when I was in high school and the lone child living with them. My extracurricular activities would often run until

7:00 or 8:00 p.m., the first imposition of distance between myself and my family. Now that his kids are all out of the house, Dad performs Sinatra at karaoke in Arizona. My father does karaoke.

I cannot sing. Or play the piano. I quit choir in elementary school because I found it boring. The piano in our house was an artifact, not an instrument. Despite knowing my siblings my entire life, I have no idea what any of them sound like when they sing. Not even "Happy Birthday." When you have three older siblings, they all sing "Happy Birthday," and they all blend together around the table because all you can focus on is the cake in front of you.

You don't pay attention because you hear them every day. You don't pay attention because their voices are more familiar than your own. You don't pay attention because you are eight and there is cake with your name on it. Then one of them gets an eating disorder and you stop having birthday cake. Then one of them gets cancer and you forget to sing "Happy Birthday."

As the years drag on and your sister begins to look more like a skeleton and your brother follows suit, you start to pay attention to the color of their thinning hair and the shape of their eyes sunken into their heads and the fact that you aren't even sure what color their eyes are.

As birthdays pass without song or celebration, you start to pay attention to the pallor that has set into your siblings' skin and the circles under their eyes that are showing up on your mother's face now too. You start to pay attention to how they draw with pastels that you can't touch and how they won't let you shake their snow globe.

But you were nine and you wanted birthday cake. You were eleven and your parents didn't explain. You were fifteen and you were studying. You were eighteen and everyone was gone. You want to remember every detail of their lives, but, twenty years later, they're all alive and well and, as you find yourself researching chemotherapy and feeding tubes, you realize all you remember is that they were dying.

Literature: A+

I noticed the sparrow while reading a book my sophomore English teacher had suggested I look at over the summer. The bird sat on our patio table, impassive, as if it belonged there. I peered up every few minutes to watch it. Each time, I expected it to be gone, to have fluttered into the sky to disappear forever. But it didn't move.

Even as I flung the sliding glass doors open—compelled to investigate why something that could fly would sit so long—it stayed still. I crept over to the table and extended my hand to touch it. I imagined it would propel itself into obscurity to live in the realm above our world—the unknown freedom of flight that humans can only simulate. As my fingers hovered above it, it still didn't move. My mother came out of the house and said it was probably injured.

It would die.

The sparrow hopped away from me across the table, bouncing inefficiently, flapping its wings as it did so. The left wing was heavy, lacking the flit that is so characteristic of tiny birds. The broken wing sent the bird in a circle, pivoting around an invisible obstacle, until it hopped back toward my hand.

I scooped up the bird and he nestled in my palm. His chest moved in and out as his wing flailed about, trying to return him to the sky. Eventually, the sparrow stopped, resigned to the fact that all he could do was breathe. I stroked his feathers gently, worried the oils of human hands could ruin them. My breathing slowed with his—my body impassive, as if it belonged there, with this bird. I sobbed, commanding tears from deep inside myself. My mother kept an eye on me from her post inside. The sparrow rested in my hand until his last breath, which could have been fifteen minutes or two hours later. I felt the sudden weight of his flightless body in my palm and my tears slowed.

He had been extinguished.

I placed the bird under a rose bush and went inside.

"It died," I said to my mom, sniffling, with a dried wall of water on my face. "It couldn't fly. And it died."

She hugged me and said, "You should wash your hands."

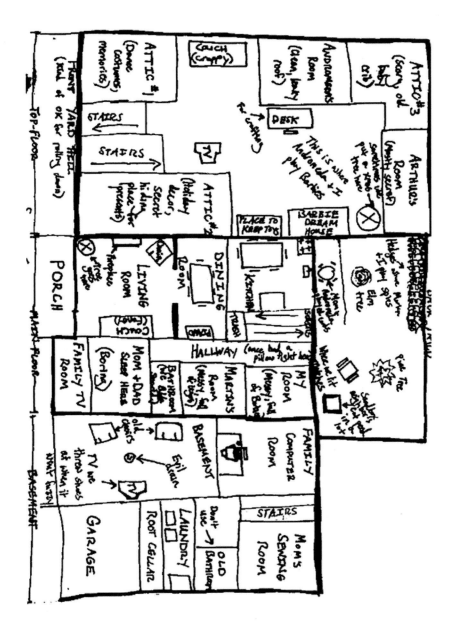

Figure 1. Childhood home as told by child who played with a lot of Barbies

Quiet

The lowest levels of the New York City subway house the rats: scavengers, harbingers of disease, rodents relegated to the depths of darkness. A few feet above them walk the humans: New Yorkers, known for their toughness, self-assigned to the underground.

Silence is a rarity here. Bars in New York remain open until 4:00 a.m. Yoga studios open at 6:00 a.m. Bodegas cover the in-between. Public transit runs endlessly to keep up with the city's workers, drinkers, and worker-outers. The rats run endlessly to escape the trains. Humans run endlessly to escape themselves.

New York is the clichéd mugger demanding "everything you got." Give up your living space for convenience. Give up human connection for thousands of coats brushing against you in winter. Give up your unobstructed landscape for underwear ads. Give up your restful quiet for the screech of train tracks.

I am drawn to New York City because I can exist in a constant state of panic here. Panic about trivial things: I can throw my self-loathing onto the cracked sidewalk that tripped me; I can combat loneliness with a latte from any one of five coffee shops in my radius; I can displace my inadequacy onto subway train departing the station without me. I exist most often in that moment of suspension—waiting. Standing on a platform, having watched the bright green "G" of a train fade into the darkness, rats trailing behind, I pause. Mundanity and fear invade my brain. *Oh, my god I'm staring at that guy with the burn scars on his face. I wasn't trying to stare; I just looked up at the wrong time and was surprised. But I'm still staring. Stop staring! Oh God now he knows I think he knows I'm staring. Quick! Look down the tunnel for the train. You know it's not coming, but you need to look somewhere. You can't look straight ahead.*

My mind races, but it keeps me from the thoughts that live deeper, the thoughts that run with the rats into the darkness. It's when I pause—when I am no longer on alert—that I realize how alone I am. Like most New Yorkers, I can't stop moving.

This constant arousal serves as a distraction, but eventually fades, leaving the same emptiness one might feel after a drinking binge. People can even die from the lack of stimulation. Dr. Curt Richter subjected rats to intense anxiety and discovered something he called *parasympathetic overshoot*. Essentially, it's calming down too quickly after immense stress. Humans—and many animals—have a sympathetic nervous system and a parasympathetic nervous system. The sympathetic nervous system triggers our "fight or flight" response. It raises the heart rate and sends a surge of adrenaline through the body. It's flooring the gas pedal while driving. The parasympathetic nervous system lowers the heart rate and returns the body to normal after intense anxiety. It's more like the gradual release of the gas followed by a steady push of the break.

Richter's experiment involved capturing wild rats—which he characterized as "fierce, aggressive, and suspicious; [...] constantly on the alert for any avenue of escape..."—and subjecting them to various stresses like subduing the rats, trapping them in velvet bags, and trimming their whiskers. After all this, the rats had to swim—rats don't like to swim. Researchers expected the lab rats to die right away in the water because they weren't used to this kind of stress. They thought the lab rats would get so overwhelmed, their sympathetic nervous systems would over-activate, as if flooring the gas and crashing into a building. The expectation was that the rats' heart rates would spike and kill them.

But the results surprised Richter. The wild rats fared far worse than the lab rats. All the wild rats died in the water within 15 minutes whereas the lab rats took hours to die. And it wasn't overstimulation that killed them. It was the opposite: the rats died from low heart rates, like slamming the breaks too quickly then being crushed by an airbag. Richter called it hopelessness. After so much intense stress, their parasympathetic nervous systems kicked in to calm them, as if accepting there was nothing left to fight for. They overcompensated because of the level of stress and stopped their hearts.

All the rats eventually gave up and died, but the lab rats clung to life much longer. Not used to living as prey or scavenging trash pizza, the lab rats swam on to the same death, colored with a drop more optimism. Either way, with only water around them, the rats stopped fighting when they finally calmed down.

In general, New Yorkers get by as well as the rats below them. Manhattan is an island built, in part, from garbage. Surrounded by water, the people of New York City keep moving to fight the same sense of hopelessness as Richter's rats. Although I likely won't die of heart failure when I cross the Hudson River, I, like many anxious and depressed pragmatists rooted in New York, have a hard time seeing beyond the water.

My fight for my life is a metaphysical one. But I often wonder at what point my own hopelessness would take over. I'm not sure I have the optimism to keep pushing when I'm *not* fighting for survival. I am aware of what I give up living here—space, quiet, disposable income, certainty—but I can't relinquish the distraction. When I can no longer blame the train for my anguish or battle depression with a midnight delivery order, I am left to face myself and the fears that scurry beneath the tedious worry.

When the train departs, I am left in silence. But it's the noise that keeps me swimming.

Stellar Remnants

This morning, my freelance boyfriend told me he found a full-time girlfriend.

He wrote me a Facebook message. It was the same way our relationship had begun. Our casual arrangement unfolded into a two-year span of roughly once-a-month dates, varying from dinner and a movie to museum visits to the Philharmonic in Central Park.

It occurs to me that this was the most serious relationship I've ever had.

As I read this message, I am downloading Phil Collins songs and playing them on repeat. I hate Phil Collins. I hate Phil Collins, but he seems to be articulating something I cannot: why I feel like all the blood and air and water has been sucked from my body.

When I saw Ben six weeks ago, I told him, "I've been calling you my 'freelance boyfriend.'"

"I like that," he said.

"It's good, right? We're not exclusive, but kind of consistent. We have no, um, 'contractual' obligation to each other, but if I needed you for, say, a wedding, I feel like I could call you."

"Yeah. I even have a tux. Let's do it!"

"You know," I admitted, "I'd been wondering if I should stop seeing you." Ben had told me he didn't want a girlfriend and I wasn't the woman to change his mind. "But," I continued, "I listed all the pros and cons and I'd either be sad now or sad later. So, I decided to stop worrying about it and just enjoy what we are. Whatever that is."

"You should understand: no matter how much I like you and I like spending time with you and no matter how much I may even love you, I'm…I'm looking for something perfect. I'm looking…" he fumbled for an example, "for the… Taj Mahal."

I wish I'd pointed out that the Taj Mahal is a mausoleum.

I also wish I'd said something about the "may even love you" comment, but I worried he'd meant it hypothetically. As a kid, I liked answers, even bad ones. I curated an acute pessimism, always assuming the worst outcome, as if to get a head start on disappointment. I was unwilling to exist in possibility or ambivalence–but I had never been faced with an "I love you," even a "may even love you." So, I chose to live in the possibility that he did love met–hat we could continue endlessly like this.

In my silence he said, more to himself than to me, "I've had it twice before and that might be all I get. I'm just not sure it's even out there."

He was looking for the kind of love that he wasn't sure existed–the kind of love I am almost certain doesn't exist for me.

"You make me happy," I said.

"You make me happy, too."

With him, my insecurity and anxiety evaporated, condensing into an easy vulnerability. In his absence, I felt something new–an exquisite longing, a desire without urgency or anguish–I missed him. Together we were happy. Apart, we were human.

Our conversation that night shifted to a book about U.S. history, which ignited both our libidos and, as we moved to his bedroom, he told me he hadn't jerked off to anyone other than me in months. I said the same went for me, but, you know, with him.

"Well, except Chris Hemsworth, occasionally," I said. He laughed.

"Oh yeah, me too," he said. I laughed as he kissed my neck.

The next afternoon, he left for a two-week trip to Italy; I left letting myself be comfortable with the unknown. After all, he had a tux waiting for me.

We made plans to go to the ballet a few weeks after he returned. His birthday passed in that time, and he hinted at wanting nude pictures, a recurrent jest of ours. When a man tells you he's masturbated to you exclusively for months, well…you know. I sent a pastiche of photos including one where I put birthday bows on my breasts.

He cancelled our ballet plans because he was going out of town but told me he wanted to reschedule. We texted winky faces and slightly dirty things and I thought we were going to see each other soon…

But a week later, I'm reading a Facebook message informing me he has a girlfriend.

As soon as I'd chosen to embrace ambivalence, I got a finite answer. Like the sudden shift from Halloween to Christmas-all-the-time that happens every year—that I know happens every year—yet am never ready for. I wake up each

November first surprised by the bomb of holiday joy and love that has exploded all over New York City. It is Christmas and I knew it was coming, but holy shit it was Halloween yesterday and now it's Christmas. What happened to Thanksgiving? What happened to November? It's not even that Halloween means so much, but it's gone now, and I don't have time to mourn it. I am assailed by Santa heads and cranberry garlands and Salvation Army bellringers, and I am alone again, completely.

I have lost a person that meant something to me. I have lost one of the first people I wanted to mean something to me.

I am not ready for this. But I am supposed to be ready for this.

Perhaps years of vigilant pessimism have exhausted my defense mechanisms. When you grow up as the youngest of four children, two of them sick with physical and mental illness, you are the bottom of the family triage. You learn to pull yourself together, to improvise in solitude, because there won't be time to grieve.

A key rule of improvisational theater is to always say "Yes, and…" This is how my mother catered to my siblings. Her days were spent running between nutritionist appointments for Andromeda and chemotherapy for Arthur. In improv, if your scene partner puts you on a sinking ship, you go with it while the audience laughs. My fourth-grade self was a willing and silent observer of my brother and sister's impending disasters. Behind the scenes, though, I crafted my own theatrics, inventing personalities, relationships, and unscripted lives for my Barbies. Through them, I tried to understand what love might be like if it were allowed to run wild, unchained by meal plans and chemo sessions. I played director to inanimate objects, testing scenarios like an emotional algorithm.

INT. UPSTAIRS PLAY AREA - DAY

    SISTER'S BARBIE (played by ANDROMEDA, age 13), wears a floor-length glittery blue evening gown, looks at herself in an invisible mirror in an invisible house.

MARYANN'S BARBIE (played by MARYANN, age
6), dressed in something boring, bounces
over to Sister's Barbie with imaginary
cookies.

                    MARYANN'S BARBIE
              I just baked cookies.
              Do you want some?

                    SISTER'S BARBIE
            No thanks, I'm on a diet.

Maryann's Barbie lies down.

"What's a diet?" I asked.

"Oh, it's where you eat just good stuff, like a lot of vegetables."

"Oh," I considered this and dismissed the concept as being irrelevant to me. "Can my Barbie wear the blue dress now?"

"No. My Barbie has to go to a party," Andromeda said.

"Can my Barbie come to the party?"

"I guess," my sister shrugged.

We set our Barbies aside to save the effort of scripting the party and watch TV instead.

Playing Barbies became a solitary activity after that, myself the omniscient narrator of my own curiosities. When Andromeda got sick and stopped playing with me entirely a year or two later, I exerted supreme control over BarbieWood.

My inventory included dozens of Barbies, but only two Kens: Blond Ken and Brunette Ken. Blond Ken was the real catch, though. Each came packaged with a bathing suit, but my sister's hand-me-down toys included one faded tuxedo that didn't quite fit either plastic man.

INT. 10-YEAR-OLD MARYANN'S BEDROOM FLOOR -
DAY

BARBIE wears a silver evening gown and ponytail. She greets THERESA (Hispanic Barbie)— wearing the glittery blue dress — SKIPPER (teen Barbie), STACY (tween Barbie), and BRUNETTE KEN (boy Barbie). All sit at a table made from an upside-down shoebox.

> BARBIE
> Stacy, how was school today?

> STACY
> Great! I got As on all my tests and I'm going to do some extra credit!

> THERESA
> Congratulations!
> *Made up Spanish congratulations*

> SKIPPER
> And *I* got into Harvard!

INT. NEXT TO SHOEBOX - LATER

BARBIE and BRUNETTE KEN stand millimeters away from each other, gaze into each other's giant cartoon eyes.

                BRUNETTE KEN
        You're so beautiful.

                BARBIE
        I know. Tell me more
        things   about   how
        great I am.

                BRUNETTE KEN
        You are as pretty as
        the   stars   and
        smarter   than
        Einstein.

Barbie smiles, tilts her head.

Ken lifts his arm up into the air to hold
Barbie. He smashes his face into hers.

They rub genitals together and fall asleep.

INT. MARYANN'S BEDROOM FLOOR – "DAY"

Barbie and Brunette Ken come home from
work.

                BRUNETTE KEN
            I'm in love with
            Theresa.

Maryann smashes Brunette Ken with Barbie.

Barbie calls BLOND KEN.

My dialogue may have improved over the years, but the story arc was generally the same. Improvised from my assumptions of my siblings' eventual absence, these play sessions always resulted in the same script: one in which love was impermanent.

When my friends came over and wanted to play with Barbie, Skipper, and the gang, I'd steer them away from these storylines and try to impress them with sexual absurdism instead. I'd incite my friends' laughter as we posited sex positions that no adults could possibly perform. We made Barbie have sex with one of her horses; we made the horses have sex with each other; we made Barbie have sex with Barbie; and Barbie with Barbie with Ken. Once, I slammed together Barbie and Ken into the adventurous 69, unaware that it was an actual sexual position. It was repulsive and fascinating and resulted in giggle fits tapered by our mutual embarrassment. When I tried this with Ben a decade and a half later, my reaction wasn't much different, although I grasped the logic behind it. He was my Blond Ken. We spent our time together being naked—shedding our clothes, our inhibitions, our outer layers—and giving equally of ourselves. Most of the time, anyway.

I inherited objects from my sister and used them as agents of my fantasies, a way to fulfill my desires without drawing attention from the more pressing concerns of my family. I could hide in the walls of Barbie's dream house, which were constructed from my brothers' series of thin hardcover books about dinosaurs. I tented each volume, aligning them to build bedroom walls so Barbie could cry, or write novels, or have sex with Blond Ken. Sometimes, I would sit in her house with her, crying in front of extinct creatures. (There, in front of Archaeopteryx, we had some privacy.) I was alone, free to command love by making it up as I went along. As I aged, and my siblings still had not passed away, I laid to rest my dolls. My interest in animate people, however, also waned, leaving me with the only great constant in my life: myself.

In psychoanalysis, it's a common exercise to think of people as objects and what those things represent in your life. My inner circle has been repeatedly recycled, like my childhood dolls. I've never met anyone outside of my immediate family that I thought I would know more than two or three years. Even my siblings, parents, and I are spread across five states and two coasts, connected by infrequent phone calls and even rarer visits. My parents once remodeled a portion of their house in the time that passed between conversations. I try not to be seen as an object. But I compare people to toys.

I thought Ben would be no different; I assumed I would grow bored of him in the way I grow bored of so many people—but he knew how to draft my play scripts along with me.

```
INT. BEN'S LIVING ROOM - 2:30
a.m.

BEN and MARYANN face each other
on the couch, their faces two
inches apart.

                 BEN
          Is it weird that
          I'm       really
          turned   on   by
          intellectual
          discussions with
          you?

Ben   leans   closer   to
Maryann.

               MARYANN
          (rapid, excited)
          No!   Actually,
          it's kind of a
          relief to hear
          you   say   that
          because    I've
          thought  exactly
          the same thing.
          When we tried to
```

```
watch Star Trek
that   one   time,
you paused it to
talk about split
infinitives  and
I    thought   you
were  so  sexy  I
just      started
making  out  with
you.
```

```
Ben   smiles.   They   smash   faces
together.
```

I spent my life awaiting disappointment—waiting for my brothers to rip my dolls' heads off; waiting for the news that my sister was back in the hospital; waiting for my brother's cancer to return—but I thought I'd have the chance to have more conversations with Ben, to hear him talk about constellations and how he used to know the capitals of every country.

Instead of absorbing the moments I had with my brother and sister, I loved my siblings because I was told to. I withheld from myself all the joy that loving another person might include. My memories of Arthur and Andromeda were collected at the end of each day, passing through short-term memory in the prefrontal cortex, stopping briefly in the frontal lobe—where emotions are processed—and perhaps skimming the fear and aggression center in the amygdala on their way to be filed in the hippocampus; from there, these memories could be recalled as fragmented fact. I only knew how to love as I loved the toys I would eventually dispose of—the artifacts of my childhood. We can admire and value artifacts—enjoy and cherish them even—but we cannot love them. I cannot be loved because I do not know how to give it.

Encoded as memory, love existed for me to be reviewed and applied in case of the unfamiliar. It was purely logical; I could preempt death and tragedy. I prepared for loss as I would a hurricane: sandbags, food stores, and a feeling of superiority. That, or evacuation. Though no amount of preparedness can prevent a natural disaster. We collectively bawled at the end of *Titanic*, knowing the ship sank before the trailers played. I know that Romeo and Juliet die, but does that make Baz Luhrmann's version any less tragic when Leo drinks the poison? I've watched Leonardo DiCaprio die dozens of times; by this point, I've come to expect it, but am I any less distraught every time it happens? I hate Phil Collins but am still unburdening every tear in my body at the sentiments in his numerous pop hits.

All my insecurities and anxieties have returned in a waterfall of despair—the waterfall that started yesterday when I was trapped in a dress that shrunk in the wash, but I was determined to squeeze into anyway. I had the zipper halfway up, but then it wouldn't move. I struggled for ten minutes, thinking it would suffocate me in the process. Because I loved that dress. I will always love that dress, even if it almost killed me.

If only I had died. If only it had killed me, and I had never seen that message. He would have wondered what happened to me. Maybe he'd post one of those creepy messages that people leave on dead people's Facebook walls—or maybe he wouldn't have said anything.

INT. BEN'S LIVING ROOM - 3:14 a.m.

Maryann sits on Ben's lap on the couch, her arms draped around his neck.

                    MARYANN
          When   I   was,
          like,   three,   I
          would beg my mom
          to   bring   home
          the   Kevin
          Costner version
          of   *Robin   Hood*
          from   my   dad's
          video store. And

she let me watch
it *every day*.

                    BEN
Ooh,   should   I
play the song?

Maryann shifts; Ben leaps to the keyboard in his
living room. He plays something but stops.

                    BEN (CONT'D)
That's   not
right.

                    MARYANN
I   watched   it
when   I   was   a
teenager   and   I
was   like   'Mom,
why   would   you
let   me   watch
this?' She asked
if I remembered
any of it, which
I didn't.

Ben plays *Everything I Do.* Both smile.

                    BEN
That's it!

```
            MARYANN
            (sighing)
 I know I'm going
 to be really sad
 when this ends…
 But I'm glad I'm
 here right now.


              BEN
 You  don't  have
 to be sad.
```

I smiled and kissed him, even though he was wrong, because I didn't know how to say what I really wanted to say.

Although, I'm beginning to believe I can learn.

Star Child: A One-Woman Show

The stage is bare. A screen behind it for projections, a stool on one side, and a small, round table with three chairs on the other. We open with a spotlight on Maryann, sitting on the stool.

MARYANN: (*as if mid-conversation*) Oh I've been fine. Busy. Working a lot. Saw a good movie. Coming to terms with my mother's alcoholism… 'Coming to terms.' Like I'm making a contract with myself. *Yes, this happened. Yes, this is my life. Yes, I will pay the balance off in full.*…I can't really say she's an alcoholic. I'm not a doctor or therapist. But…I can't really remember days when she didn't drink. But memories are fallible. The brain sees things all the time that aren't there. (*beat*) That's a premise of Gestalt psychology. It's called closure—funny terminology, huh? It's like…if I drew a circle and erased a little bit of it, you'd see it and go 'yeah, that's a circle.' We don't need every detail to understand.

But that's also kind of the problem, isn't it? Because what if the part of the circle I erased was because I was drawing a Venn diagram? Doesn't really leave space for ambivalence.

When I was a kid, she always had wine at dinner. In middle school, she started at four. In high school…three sometimes. Sometimes noon. I remember her going through this phase of buying Costco bottles of tonic water and drinking gin and tonics on summer afternoons. Sitting on the patio, drinking gin and tonics, like…like…a flamboyant Hemingway. Who doesn't write. So, like an alcoholic without the lasting literary contributions.

(*Maryann walks across the stage.*)

But her real love is wine. She's been pretty faithful to it. Once she opens a bottle, the glass doesn't empty until the bottle does. She buys the bottles in bulk, which is smart, really. She knows she's gonna drink it.

SLIDE 1:

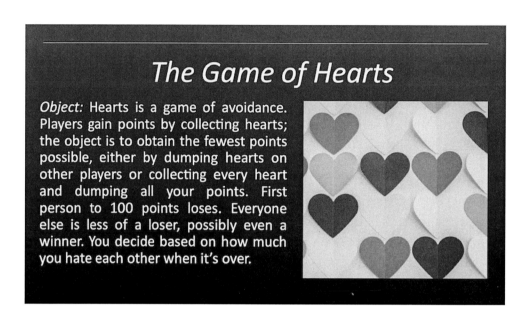

MARYANN: I went to preschool at random. I had a stay-at-home mom, which removed the need for regular babysitters—well, apart from the television.

But I loved preschool.

I remember my first visit there. My small hands dangled near my mother's fingers as she pulled me around. It was a mystical realm with a giant pit sheathed in blue carpet where people the same size as me played with puzzle pieces the same size as them. They built castles together with their tiny hands and squealed in rhythmic glee.

I wanted to let go completely, to rush down the carpeted stairs and be with the other tiny people. But I couldn't give up my grip, no matter how tenuous it was.

I was like a worldly aunt, flying in and out of school at the whims of my parents. Mom would drop me off sporadically, abandoning me to drown in whatever arts and crafts project everyone else had been working on for a week.

(Maryann moves to center stage.)

Before the holiday pageant, my teacher told us to bring milk cartons so we could perform some spell to transform them into lanterns. My family of six only purchased milk in plastic gallon jugs because my brothers guzzled dairy products like diesel trucks. I had never seen a cardboard milk container. I spent the week supervising my family's milk consumption so I could deliver a container to my magical preschool teacher and follow through on my lantern.

I insisted the plastic jug was what my teacher had asked for, despite my mother's hesitations. When I returned to preschool on the day of the pageant—having stayed most of the week at home as I usually did—it turned out everyone had been making lanterns out of cardboard cartons. They cut the sides out and replaced them with tissue paper. It seemed the toddlers had also decapitated the cartons and slid flashlights inside of them to illuminate the paper walls.

(*Holds up sample lantern; turns flashlight on to demonstrate.*)

The teachers accommodated me, as they always did. My empty plastic jug retired to the trashcan, and someone found me a spare lantern. I stood in the front row, still small among my peers, and sang *Silent Night* at the bottom of a blue pit while parents gazed on.

I can't remember if my mother stayed for the pageant.

SLIDE 2:

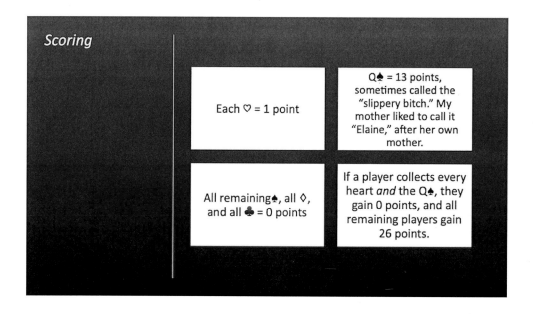

(Maryann walks to the table and sits. She pulls out a deck of cards and begins shuffling, then stops.)

MARYANN: Psychologist Harry Harlow took newborn rhesus monkeys from their mothers and replaced the maternal units with cylindrical surrogates made of wire and wood. The surrogates had faces, but barely looked like parents beyond serving as milk-bottle-holders. Harlow made two sets of "mothers." One was bare wire, and one was covered in terry cloth. In one condition, only the wire mother held a bottle for the infant monkeys to nurse. In the other, only the terry cloth mother had a bottle. Regardless of where the bottle was, the monkeys spent most of their time clinging to the terry cloth mothers. I imagine them grasping the fibers with their tiny fingers, absorbing whatever infinitesimal specks of affection they could.

(Walks across stage.)

As adults, these monkeys—all reared with the basic needs of survival, but in the absence of a real mother—were emotionally unstable, aggressive, and neglectful—or abusive—of their own children. They displayed erratic sexual behavior and isolated themselves from other monkeys. Harlow constructed a literal monkey playground where his deprived rhesus infants sidelined themselves.

(Maryann shuffles the deck of cards, spreads them out, does a few card tricks etc. as she talks.)

SLIDE 3:

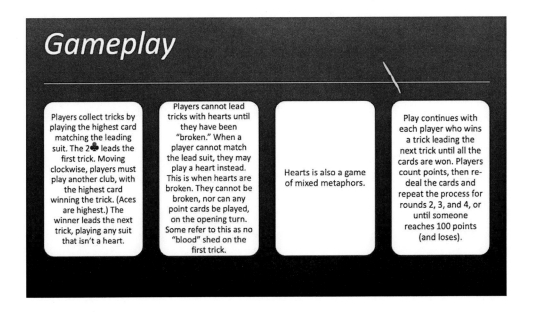

MARYANN: Harlow, an iconoclast of the time, wanted to make the point that caregiving requires more than providing food and shelter; that humans need to be nurtured. His enormously unethical experiments, which ignited the animal liberation movement and led to more stringent ethical standards in the psychological community, were also immensely important. It was Harlow who pioneered what we often take for granted today: love and affection are human necessities.

SLIDE 4:

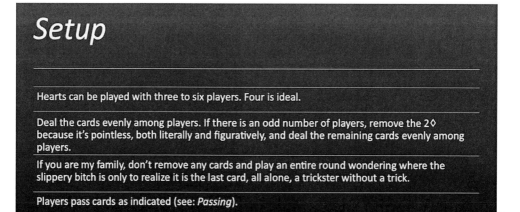

> **Setup**
>
> Hearts can be played with three to six players. Four is ideal.
>
> Deal the cards evenly among players. If there is an odd number of players, remove the 2◊ because it's pointless, both literally and figuratively, and deal the remaining cards evenly among players.
>
> If you are my family, don't remove any cards and play an entire round wondering where the slippery bitch is only to realize it is the last card, all alone, a trickster without a trick.
>
> Players pass cards as indicated (see: *Passing*).
>
> After passing is complete, the player with the 2♣ plays first (see: *Gameplay*).

(Maryann deals all the cards to four imaginary players.)

MARYANN: Harlow's groundbreaking maternal deprivation experiment took place in 1958, more than 40 years after the invention of the tank, 19 years after the first helicopter, and 13 years after the United States dropped an atomic bomb on Japan.

My parents were born in 1953.

(Maryann sits on the stool.)

I was born in 1989. I was born en-caul, inside a bubble of amniotic fluid, like a chunk of pear suspended in Jell-O. At least that's what I thought. I Googled it and it's more like a set of tiny arms and legs stuffed in a murky Ziploc bag.

Being born with a caul—that's any remnant of amniotic membrane around a baby's head—happens in about one in 80,000 births. En-caul births,

like mine, are slightly rarer and usually happen with premature babies. (proudly)
But *I* was seven hours late.

(*Maryann stands*)

Historically, cauls held supernatural significance, most often as signs of good luck or greatness. Some believed luck would follow the "bearer of the caul;" others thought it would pass on to their offspring.

My mother only knows this fact about me because the midwife who delivered me told her. Mom had the option to break the water—making the birth more difficult for me—or keeping it intact and making the birth more difficult for her. "Don't hurt the baby," she said, a veteran child-bearer with three prior vaginal births to her credit.

In the Middle Ages, sailors thought cauls would protect you from drowning. Sometimes, they were removed by a midwife and sold as charms.

(*Maryann puts on a set of water wings and sits back down.*)

Even today, some people born with a caul believe they are destined for greatness...

(*Maryann puts on a paper crown.*)

...or have special powers like the ability to read minds or speak to ghosts. There are some very cult-y looking webpages for "star children," en-caul babies-turned-adults who discuss their earthly burdens.

My mother used to speak to ghosts. (*pantomiming*) She would lift a pen, as if possessed by spirits, and her hand moved across paper, scribbling incoherently.

In Romanian folklore, those born with a caul would become vampires after death, doomed to live immortally in isolated dark. I'm partial to that one.

(*Begins taking off crown, then water wings as she speaks.*)

SLIDE 5:

My mother would scold my father for not waking her up in the morning because she was afraid she would be "sucked into her dreams," as if the spirit world beckoned. I inherited her emotional distress, and my father's ability to understand it. I was born in a literal bubble, and, like the other star children, I can see the significance of being born inside your own boundary.

(*Maryann walks to the table and scoops up the playing cards she dealt. She sits.*)

For years, I thought my mother might be schizophrenic. It was a comfort, in some ways, to think she couldn't help it. As a matter of genetics, it was kind of scary.

SLIDE 6:

Dad ╲ Mom	**Mental Illness**	**Mental Illness**
sanity	Ms	Ms
sanity	Ms	Ms

MARYANN: I'm at my best in the cerebral. Other than sadness, I can rarely identify an emotion when I have one.

Two parts of the brain control most of our emotions: the amygdala and the frontal cortex. The amygdala controls our most basic human drives—aggression…fear…sex. The frontal cortex controls our most complex. It doesn't completely develop until our early twenties.

I thought everyone in my family had brown eyes, like me, until I was in my early twenties. During one of our rare visits as adults, I noticed my brother Arthur—my sibling closest geographically and furthest in age—had green eyes. Did I miss it because it wasn't important? Or because I couldn't let myself look too closely?

SLIDE 7:

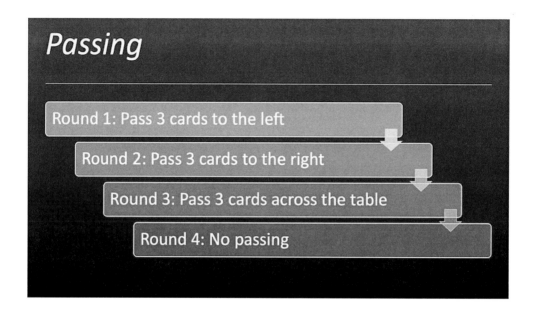

(Maryann deals the cards again as she speaks, acting out as she explains.)

MARYANN: They're called tricks, by the way. Each time you throw down a card, another player throws another card, the next player throws another... and whoever has the highest card matching the first suit played takes the trick. The thing is... usually people don't *want* tricks.

(She holds up the cards in her hand, revealing the Queen of Spades, then shuffles them again.)

MARYANN: Our house was always company-ready, though we rarely had people over. The living room and dining room were pristine, an exhibit on the suburban middle-class nuclear family. Our disarray was tucked into the corners of our basement. Hidden in the back of the house, mine and Martin's rooms were two microcosms of childish chaos. But we were always prepared for public appearances. I was groomed and polite in public, like our immaculate living room. But in the isolation of my bedroom—there, behind the safety of walls—I lived in indulgence. Toys and clothes everywhere. I burrowed a path from my door to my bed. Martin and I were gluttonous, both with appetites for junk food and toys. The gravity of our ill siblings upstairs pulled our parents out of our orbit. We compensated by engineering our own worlds, ones our mother ignored. I never had to clean my room because only I existed there, a little astronaut tending my own space station.

SLIDE 8:

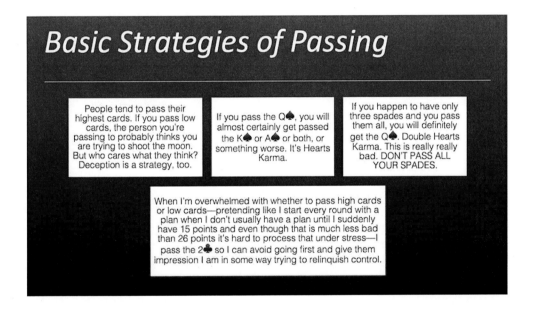

MARYANN: My mother was the inverse of the house she looked after. Disorder exploded from her. From her Tourette's twitches to her sequin shirts and floor-length skirts with cowgirls and lime-green polka dot dress, she was flamboyant, unmistakable. Like Polaris or the aurora borealis. But like the home she kept, my mother's darkest messes lived under the stairs. The basement housed her sewing room, strewn with thread and fabric scraps. It was where she obsessed. She cycled through hobbies until she and my father retired to Arizona. Sewing remained through it all, a way to stitch together mixed-up pieces. But when I was in high school, she started knitting. She made scarves and hats and scarves and hats for all of us. She made mittens and gloves in more and more complicated patterns; gloves two sizes too large for my always-tiny hands. Cooking fatty meals for us became the hobby du jour after my sister moved out. She made cheesy things that we could never finish and complimented herself furiously at each meal. No one was a bigger fan of my mother than my mother.

The obsession to rule them all, though, was alcohol. It was *her* Polaris, a broken compass pointing her further away from reality. When I'd finally said the words out loud—*I don't know if I love my mother. I'm not sure anymore if I ever did*— I felt something slip out of me, like that gooey amniotic fluid. I felt lighter. When my therapist said the words back to me—*Oh my god, my mother is an alcoholic*—I just thought, *yeah. Sounds right.* I didn't need to defend her.

I started seeing a psychiatrist in my late twenties and in a 45-minute evaluation, she solved a couple decades worth of puzzles for me. She said my mother's delusions—often in the mornings—were probably a result of *delirium tremens.* From alcohol withdrawal.

SLIDE 9:

IT ALL MAKES SENSE

(*Maryann walks to the stool and sits. Then speaks.*)

MARYANN: My mother is an alcoholic. Well, I *think* my mother is an alcoholic. I'm pretty sure she's an alcoholic. She buys wine in six-packs and guzzles glasses to celebrate afternoon's arrival. She drinks. She complains. She tells us *all I believe in is love.* She cries. She drinks. And when her son asks her a question she doesn't want to answer she accuses: *all of you just attack me.* She cries. She drinks. And complains my father doesn't understand her. She sobs. She worries that he doesn't worry. She says he doesn't understand, and he agrees. No one understands because she speaks a different language: *love.*

How could I have denied it for so long?

SLIDE 10:

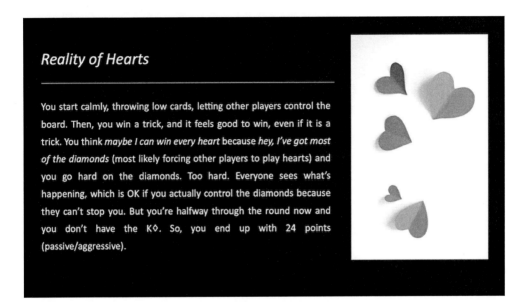

Reality of Hearts

You start calmly, throwing low cards, letting other players control the board. Then, you win a trick, and it feels good to win, even if it is a trick. You think *maybe I can win every heart* because *hey, I've got most of the diamonds* (most likely forcing other players to play hearts) and you go hard on the diamonds. Too hard. Everyone sees what's happening, which is OK if you actually control the diamonds because they can't stop you. But you're halfway through the round now and you don't have the K◊. So, you end up with 24 points (passive/aggressive).

(Lights slowly come up.)

MARYANN: My mother is a supernova. She is visible from a distance. She wears sequin tops and fist-sized jewelry and talks about how married men in her retirement community tell her how great she looks. She jokes. She tells stories. She argues. She speaks in unattached pronouns and tears—she interrupts. She tries to set her adult children up on dates with wait staff. She does victory jigs when she wins board games. She complains. And complains.

She is a burst of light. She implodes and spews energy into the space around her.

She leaves a black hole in her wake.

SLIDE 11:

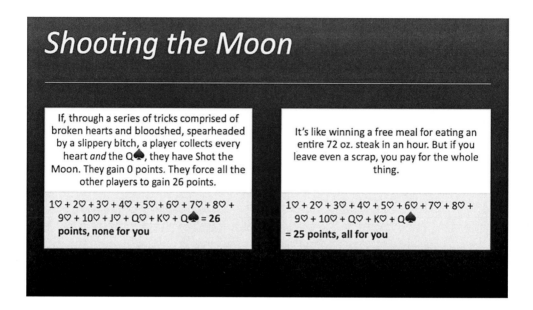

BLACK

Lights come up. Maryann is pouring coffee at the table and setting mugs out to each seat.

MARYANN: The morning after Christmas a few years ago, I woke up at my brother Arthur's house and met him in the kitchen. He and his wife were sipping coffee. I'd rolled out of bed around 10. Arthur turned to me.

"Dad called this morning," he said. "I have some bad news."

In the seconds-long pause before he delivered this news, I imagined our mother in the hospital, maybe dead. A fall by the pool with a drink in her hand.

(Maryann walks center stage, holding a cup of coffee.)

I felt…relief. She hadn't been sick, but even just imagining it, I felt some burden float off me and drift upward into the stars.

Then, I panicked. I didn't know what the news was, but in the time that extended between my brother's breaths, I wished what I had imagined were true. And I didn't feel guilty about it. But I was standing in my brother's kitchen. He would expect me to react. To be saddened, shocked, grief-stricken. And I wasn't.

"Nana died this morning," he said.

I took a second to recalculate. This made more sense. Our 95-year-old paternal grandmother had passed in her sleep. Though my moment of confusion between my imagination and reality may have registered as surprise, I wasn't shocked by this news either. Our grandmother had been in good physical health, but mental disarray. It's a fate I hope to avoid by dying early, but I've had two grandfathers live into their 80s and two grandmothers live into their 90s.

(*Cross to stage right.*)

She was the grandparent I knew best, even though we hadn't spoken in years. Nana's eyesight and memories had been fading for a decade. When I'd last spoken to her, five years earlier, she'd thought I was my father's cousin. And that my father was a teenager. My grandmother had been traveling back in time, her life erased slowly, until all the bad memories had gone, and she could die at peace.

Her husband started suffering from dementia long before my grandmother showed signs of it. My grandparents had to stop visiting us in Montana because the flight from New Jersey became too long for him; he wouldn't remember where he was mid-flight. My mother and father only visited their families in New Jersey once. I was six months old at the time. So, my memories of Grandpa, our unanimously favorite relative, were a glob of once-a-year visits until I was eleven and second-hand stories from my siblings.

Grandpa died twelve years before Nana did. I was in high school then and separated from all my grandparents by thousands of miles. My father grabbed the last seat on a flight to New Jersey to go to his father's funeral. I'd asked to go, too, but the answer was no. After my grandfather died—my first close experience with death—I asked my father if I could spend a summer with Nana. I'd wanted to feel connected to something.

I stayed with her for two weeks when I was 15. Even then, I thought it would be a great story someday: the dutiful granddaughter who was so close to her grandmother. But all I remember from that summer was that she struggled to read large print books and was happy to have me read VHS tapes so we could find movies we wanted to watch. We loved Audrey Hepburn, especially. We watched *Roman Holiday* and *Breakfast at Tiffany's*. My mom never wanted to watch *Breakfast at Tiffany's*. She didn't think it was that good. But it's basically a rite of passage, right?

I told myself I was there to be closer to my grandmother. I think what I really wanted was the appearance of caring.

My parents told me I didn't have to go to Nana's funeral. My father wasn't flying out this time, but I lived nearby, in New York City. My mom and dad have always encouraged me to steer away from their families because of the maelstroms of guilt they both produce. I wanted to go to the ceremony because my mother didn't want me to. But I didn't *want* to go at all. Funerals aren't for the dead; they're for the grieving. And I don't know how to grieve. I cried when my grandfather died because I didn't have the chance to know the man my brothers and sister and father loved so much. I grieved my own isolation.

There would have been no closure at my Nana's funeral that I didn't already have. We'd stopped talking years ago because the same biology that created me from her, erased my existence to her. She didn't know she had granddaughters. She didn't know she had children. She left this life with no memory of what she had brought into it.

I didn't go to the funeral for the same reason I don't give condolence calls. What good does it do to be reminded of the loved ones you've lost? Condolences aren't for the person grieving. They're for the person making the call. They're a point of pride, used to remind ourselves that we are good and caring people.

I am not a good and caring person. I don't need to be reminded that I haven't been close enough to another person in almost fifteen years to be upset by their loss. It took three years in therapy and two seconds imagining— hoping—my mother had died to realize just how incapable of love I am. I don't know how to love my mother. Perhaps at some point I did. But I have a suspicion my mother doesn't know how to love me either.

We learn that children and parents love each other, but what about when they don't? There's no picture book to identify that other bundle of emotions you feel toward your mentally ill mother, that tangled constellation of admiration and fear and anger and hate.

For years, I defended her, the victim of an alcoholic father, a cold and unloving mother of her own, and their tumultuous marriage. She did her best with an anorexic daughter and a son with cancer. But I failed to see my mom as a bully, twisting herself into the role of accused, when in fact my brothers and sister and I were the victims of an alcoholic mother, a cold and unloving caretaker, and her tumultuous marriage to our father. I failed to see her as the same mother she so resented. I failed to see her as my sister's devourer. I failed to see the same cold and unloving nature in myself—the kind of affection I could never inflict upon someone else.

SLIDE 12:

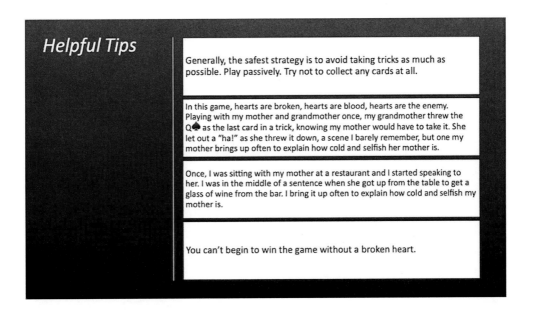

MARYANN: I learned not to love things too deeply when I was seven. My first-grade teacher had given each student a two-week old pine tree to take care of and plant.

Nearly every day after school, I pulled out our wobbly wooden stool and set it in front of the kitchen sink. My tiny arms—tiny even among my schoolmates—stretched across the sink to the window ledge. I cupped the nascent tree, in its recycled cardboard container, and held it under the spigot. Following my teacher's instructions, I lifted the faucet and watched the tap water stream into the dirt around the infant pine until I could see it trickle out the bottom of the cardboard.

I repeated the process of watering my tree for weeks. I watched it sprout a new branch, a nub of tree trunk smaller than my own fingernail.

It lived. It grew.

I asked my mother if we could plant it, as our teacher had told us to do. We could make a new tree, new life in the world. She said *we might be able to.*

I came home one day to find my tree missing. Its window ledge was barren, no trace of its little pine scent, no cardboard remnants. My mother told me it had died.

I had nurtured my tiny tree—I nurtured it, and it died.

SLIDE 13:

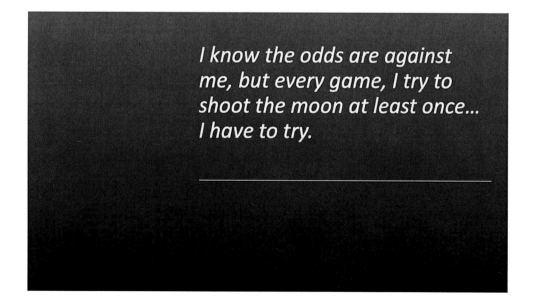

(Maryann reveals a handful of cards, with all 13 hearts and the Queen of Spades.)

MARYANN: I read an article that suggested cats may not love their owners, that they may only mimic affection and pretend to love us. I found this unsurprising, although it made me admire my cat more. It seemed more impressive if Marzipan could manipulate me than if she could genuinely love me.

When I shared my discovery with friends, they consoled me. *Oh, I'm sure your cat loves you.* I tried to explain that I didn't care. This felt familiar to me. *If I think she loves me, what's the difference?*

My friends looked at me; their faces twisted quizzically as they tried to decipher whether I was kidding. I wasn't kidding.

Maryann, they said, *of course it's different.*

It wasn't until my late twenties when I began to understand this idea. In the same way romantic comedies are not reality, reciting rote sentiments and acting out gestures of affection are not love. The idea that my cat might only need me for food and water is familiar and safe. When she climbs into my bed and nestles beside me, I wonder if either one of us is feeling anything more than a few extra degrees of body heat.

I think the first thing I ever loved was a cat. I visited an animal shelter with my third-grade class and met a neurotic one hiding in the corner of a room with dozens of the carnivorous beasts roaming freely. I asked a volunteer for the cat's name and researched the responsibilities of cat-ownership at the school library. Armed with facts and a can-do attitude, I begged my mother to take me back so she could meet Sadie, the weird cat who scratched herself from anxiety and looked like an unfinished painting: she was mostly white with three large tan and black spots, a striped tail, and a spotted calico face.

Astonished that my mother agreed to go to the animal shelter, I had no hopes of taking Sadie home. Still, getting my mom to even entertain the idea of a pet felt like an accomplishment. When we got there, I looked around the room for Sadie, but couldn't find her. I checked the door with all the cats' names on it. Sadie's name was gone. I burst into tears, my first genuine pangs of loss. She was gone and there was no time for goodbye.

Someone who worked at the shelter saw me crying and told us she didn't think Sadie had been adopted. It turned out I had fallen in love with the cat who tended to hide under cages because she was afraid of the other cats.

The employee found her behind a metal cage and pulled her out, thrusting Sadie into the air like a recovered remote control. I held the cat, her paws pressed against my skin in a gesture I understood as love but was almost certainly fear. I was a method of escape, a way out of the jungle of cats—of her own kind— where she felt so out of place.

My mother talked my father into letting me have the cat. My father agreed under the condition the cat would live in our finished basement. Within a day, my father learned that cats have no respect for human boundaries. The first night we had her, we put Sadie in the basement with a gate at the top of the stairs, which she vaulted over three times. When we turned the lights off, she cried. She let out long, empty meows. I'd never heard the sound before, but I knew it immediately: she was lonely. I snuck out of my room three times to descend into the terrifying basement that flooded in the rain and stayed with her, hoping to lull her to sleep. I knew dreams were the best distraction from loneliness.

By the next morning, the cat glided through every room of our two-story house. My mother fed her while I was at school and Sadie slept every night in my bedroom. She was pudgy when we adopted her, but she grew to be more than twenty pounds from my mother's constant feeding. I think we all understood there was some greater meaning in an obese cat next to an anorexic daughter, but none of us knew what it was. At least, we never admitted it.

It was a running joke that my mother put the work in and the cat liked me more. I think Mom needed something that needed her, even if it was only pretending. My mother has always been best reached by emotional appeal rather than reason.

"When I saw how upset you were when you thought she'd been adopted," she told me once, "I had to get the cat." I wonder if she recognized something in me then, her quiet daughter who played with stuffed animals more than human friends. I think my mother knew I was like her; I think she adopted the cat hoping I could learn to love something.

After my first semester of college, my parents picked me up at the Phoenix airport and took me to the Cheesecake Factory where they told me Sadie was dead.

"Well, in November, I let her out and I didn't realize she hadn't come back inside," my mother started on the verge of tears.

"We looked for her and asked everyone in the neighborhood if they saw her. But she'd been acting kind of strange for a couple weeks," my dad added. "She was old."

I understood what they were telling me, but I couldn't understand why they both seemed so upset.

Dad said, "We think she probably got eaten by a coyote."

At least a coyote got a hearty meal, I thought.

"We wanted to wait for you to finish finals and everything, so we didn't tell you until now," my mom said, fighting tears.

It was one of the most thoughtful things I could remember my parents doing. I wish they'd been right. I thought I'd miss her more when I left for college. But as I discovered with everything else I'd abandoned, my heart hadn't made room for anything more than blood. I wish it had hurt when they told me my childhood pet—the first thing I'd ever cried over—was gone. I wish my heart had broken a little. Maybe some space would have opened inside me.

I took a bite of my salad and shrugged.

"I mean, she was old."

Maryann pushes the table aside and sets up the three chairs in a row. She grabs a remote from offstage and lies across the chairs, as if they were a couch. She points the remote at audience members and pushes buttons.

MARYANN: On weekday mornings, I sometimes watched *The Price Is Right* before going to kindergarten. It was a ritual I missed as I got older and went to real school. When I would stay home sick, I drifted through channels without understanding how TV schedules worked. An accidental landing on an airing of *The Price is Right* was the only upside to missing school. At ten, I liked to guess the cost of Flintstones vitamins (expensive) and sponges (not expensive), but I struggled with concepts like thousands of dollars.

Once, in my snot-fueled academic deprivation, my mother let me stay home by myself. She stopped into the TV room to tell me she needed something from the store. She provided no further detail.

She asked if I wanted to go to the store. I liked the store. But for the first time, it seemed I had a choice. I wanted to remain in the fantasy grocery aisle that could transform Pepto Bismol into a Toyota.

"Um…I'll stay here," I said.

"Ok. I'll be gone ten minutes."

Our TV room sat on top of the garage. I felt the door vibrate beneath me as she left, in sync with the reveal of an RV in the Showcase Showdown. My electrons excited with the unbearable burden of freedom. Home. Alone. At ten. Possibilities zipped from one end of my body to the other, pure joy rushing through my developing cerebral cortex as the garage door scraped closed. *I could do anything.*

(*Maryann paces across the stage.*)

I went to the kitchen. I took two cookies and returned to my post on the couch. Nervous to lose this newly afforded liberty, I felt an obligation not to injure myself or make a mess. I'd been left alone, and I imposed my own rules. Somehow, I internalized my mother's chaos and I found myself yearning for order. The garage door disturbance was enough turmoil for the day. I was alone, just as I had always been, and I felt so small. Too helpless for an adventure.

Mom returned at some point during the next TV show. The garage vibrations upon her return depleted my excitement. She told me she was back, then descended to her sewing room. I went back to the kitchen and took three more cookies.

(*Stops pacing.*)

There's this principal in Gestalt psychology called Closure. Where you can see parts of things and complete them. You don't need all the details. But sometimes, as much as we want to define things and close them into neat little shapes—hearts and triangles and stars and circles—we just can't.

LITTLE ASTRONAUT

(Sits in the middle of the stage, cross-legged on the ground.)

On my first day of kindergarten, my mother dropped me at the end of the sidewalk outside Irving School. She didn't want me to be embarrassed by walking in with her. With my thumbs looped between my backpack straps and corduroy jumper, I walked toward the playground—I was in afternoon kindergarten, so I got to school at lunch time. Sometimes, my mom would get me McDonald's before school. I loved that. I loved chicken nuggets and spending time with my mother.

As I rounded the corner, I saw an older kid playing basketball and I realized he'd been there all day. That was so exciting to me. I hadn't even started school and I wanted to be there all day. And I think my mom knew I belonged there. She let me go, her little astronaut, ready to launch into outer space and grab the moon.

Virginity Limbo

The legal age at which one can earn a driver's license in Montana is 15 (losing out only to South Dakota for youngest driving age in the U.S.). Children could earn a learner's permit as young as 14 and a half. The argument for this: some kids needed to help on the family farm running equipment or popping into town with the pick-up truck. A year before I left for college, the state proposed a graduated license law, one where teens couldn't drive late at night and had restrictions on their number of passengers. Before 2006, teenage drivers held all the same freedoms as adults.

At the time, I was growing up in Bozeman, which looks more like a Connecticut suburb than the backdrop of a Marlboro ad. Few teens in my town earned their licenses at 15; suburban parents were reticent to turn over such a responsibility to their high school freshmen. Most kids took driver's ed at that time, though. It took place in the evenings, when my rich extracurricular life was blossoming—speech and debate, theater, Model UN, and the mishmash of clubs I never stuck with.

My parents, longstanding non-traditionalists, taught me how to drive.

> ### Durston Road
> ### Bozeman, MT
> ### August 20, 2005

My first driving lesson was with my mother. She drove me down a long stretch of field-lined roads until we discovered a cul-de-sac village where I spent an hour making left turns and reversing and braking from my treacherous 20-mile-per-hour joyride.

Hunters Way
Bozeman, MT
August 27, 2005

My father took me on my next driving lesson in our slightly less empty suburban neighborhood. He focused on user experience—braking gently and all that. Neither emphasized laws—both taught me how to drive as a driver, not as a driver's ed student. Mom told me to stay kind of in the middle of the lane because, in Montana, someone coming the other direction wasn't much of a problem. She liked to avoid parked cars by risking a brush with a moving one. My father told me to stay in my lane because he hadn't considered not doing so.

My parents explained parallel parking in basically the same way. But my mother's lack of verbs or nouns compiled with my father's driving lingo made their methods feel irreconcilable. I spent hours practicing this, having watched so many sitcom teens fail their driving tests due to a stubborn curb. Instead, I failed my first driver's test because I rolled to a graceful stop with the nose of my mom's mini-van sniffing just over the edge of the white line marking a stop sign stop. That was an automatic failure, I learned from Driver's Ed friends. Less than two minutes out of the parking lot and I'd already lost, but the instructor put me through the test anyway. She noted things like my tendency to drive in the middle of the road and my poor depth perception. My pragmatist parents suggested I practice, follow the rules for the exam, and then ignore them.

DMV
Bozeman, MT
January 6, 2006

Four months short of my 17th birthday, I passed—my second try. It was assumed I'd go away to college, so my parents saw investing in a car for me as impractical. It also narrowed the list of colleges I could apply to—all campuses had to be in an urban area where I could get around without a car. Somehow, this reduced my application list to one liberal arts college outside Portland, Oregon, four ivy league schools, and New York University. I only got into NYU. We'd vastly overshot, despite my parents' longstanding non-expectations. My father was mostly apathetic to my achievements—successes and failures elicited the same non-reactions. My mother prided herself on her lack of expectations; she was a *good mother*, she said, for not putting pressure on me to succeed. She took the same sense of pride in her children's understated birthday celebrations and her no-effort holidays. She was a *good mother*, she said, because she *wasn't like her mother*, she said. With all that self-admiration, there wasn't a lot of room for pride in any of my successes. But I kept trying.

While I waited to deploy my ejector seat and land on a coast as far away from Montana as I could get (above the Mason-Dixon line, anyway) Mom and I split custody of her minivan. Before I could drive, they'd ask my brother to pick me up from school most days. Once I'd achieved the all-American milestone of a driver's license, I could drive myself to school and leave our teenage Dodge Caravan in one of the two enormous Bozeman High School parking lots. Mom would often stay at home all day or, in the non-life-threatening spring weather, walk around town on her errands. This way, I could drive home after dark; my parents didn't like to leave the house after 5:00 p.m.

Some days, Mom needed the car. If I couldn't get a ride from a friend, most of whom lived on the other end of town, she'd ask me to walk home. Once April arrived, I didn't have so many things keeping me in the drab high-school hallways after sunset. These were the months my mother needed her car most often.

> 19th Street
> Bozeman, MT
> April 27, 2006

It was about a mile walk, a distance I cover four times over in an average city day. It wasn't treacherous. It wasn't uphill. But it was lonely. Unlike the crowded streets of New York City, with a constant flow of fellow travelers brushing by, the streets of suburban Bozeman were almost void of humanity. Parking lots and trees lined the equivalent of my hometown's Madison Avenue. Moderate traffic moved past, an underscore to my walk home, alone. It wasn't the walk itself that I so deplored, it was the emptiness of it.

I was never sure how to articulate this to my mother, though. It's hard to express shame to someone who doesn't experience it. My meek objections were usually met with the insinuation that I needed exercise. She was a *good mother*. She prided herself on not having expectations.

§

Even though it wasn't dark on these walks home, I think I was always aware of the implications of a woman walking alone. I knew about rape from an early age, I think before I even knew what sex was. In kindergarten, I learned about dinosaurs by visiting the Museum of the Rockies, home to one of the world's most complete Tyrannosaurus Rex fossils. It was discovered by Jack Horner, a paleontologist famous for his research to support the fact that T-Rex was actually a scavenger. At the age of five, I knew that this, too, was my calling: dinosaur-uncoverer and myth-debunker. Paleontologist was the first six-syllable word I learned and the first career aspiration I had, having no working knowledge of what the job entailed. I understood sex similarly: an important thing, a thing that revealed mysteries. Rape was when someone took something important away, obscured any answers. Walking home from high school in the summer, I faced the same hazards of exposure I did in the cold. A young victim, given away by her bouncing backpack and sweat-speckled brow.

I latched on to the grotesque as a kid. I devoted myself to *Law & Order.* It existed almost as long as I had. I wanted to be a police officer when I was eight, so the police investigation was my favorite part of the show. In every game of *Life,* I played with my siblings at the time, I wanted to be the poorly paid police officer living in the house that had yet to be renovated after an earthquake. We once played a round where my siblings made me take whatever career I drew and play by the rules. I was an artist making $100,000 a year and living in a four-bedroom Tudor on a tree-lined block. I threw a tantrum. I usually had to go to bed halfway through *Law & Order*, when it gave way to Sam Waterston's eyebrows trying murders in a Court of Law, or what I deemed "the Order part." Then came *Law & Order: SVU*, when I turned 11.

It was around that time my career aspirations were between actress and lawyer. As a fifth grader, I even got a role on a BBC mini-series that never aired called *Dinosaur Detectives,* fulfilling all my childhood dreams at once. I met Jack Horner who pointed to a Pepsi can with Jar Jar Binks on it and said, "that guy is an idiot," then, on camera, explained the dinosaur hatching process with a replica of a fossilized egg. I also remember shooting a scene where I was supposed to hold a raw hamburger in a bun and be interrupted in my headset before I could take a bite of it. It seemed a little dangerous to give an eleven-year-old raw beef and tell her to "pretend to eat it," but if that was the price of stardom, I was ready and willing.

Eventually, I decided I wanted to be prosecutor, a special victims' assistant district attorney specifically, like the pretty blonde woman with the glasses. I attribute my early interest in detective work to my enjoyment of puzzles and scripted television. But it's just as likely this is what engrained in me the implicit fear of rape—in college, I started taking birth control in part due to my irregular periods, in part to be safe from pregnancy in the event I was raped in an alley. New York City has almost no alleys amid it's luxury high-rises and dilapidated soon-to-be-luxury-high-rises. Bozeman had alleyways on every block. From a young age, I was astutely aware of what it meant to be penetrated.

I carried that fear for years, avoiding parties where there might be teenage boys and alcohol all through high school. Each passing year without losing my virginity, I became more afraid of sex, more afraid of the ballooning breasts my mother wouldn't let me forget, more afraid of driving too fast veering off the road, and more afraid of being the little girl I might crash into.

> ## "Bedwicksburg"
> ## Brooklyn, NY
> ## Many years later

I lost my virginity when I was 24. Sometimes, I wish I waited longer. Shame is a self-fueling fire. For me, it began in unknowing—secrets hidden behind velvet curtains, silence in the face of visible illness. *What else do we not talk about?* It glowed from within, stoked by my mother's ambiguous expectations. *I'm afraid to walk home alone, but why can't I tell her?* It burned hotter as friends and acquaintances would ask things like *why don't you have a boyfriend? Are you a lesbian? Why not just have sex and get it over with?* Eventually, I did. I wanted to extinguish it and wash the ash of embarrassment away.

The first time was like trying to shove a salami into a bagel. A real New York bagel, one that's basically just a loaf of bread with a belly button. The pain was unbearable, so far beyond my expectations of "the first time hurts." It happened again the next time I tried, and the next time after that. It happened with Ben, who was the first person to accept my shame, to allow me to feel it without further judgement. But I was still so inexperienced I didn't know what was wrong, or how wrong it even was. It was crossing the white stop line again. Did it matter if I was an inch or a foot over the line? I failed anyway.

Fixing my dysfunctional vagina was first a matter of identifying the source of its delinquency. At least two gynecologists told me to "just relax." One suggested I smoke pot. Neither had an answer as to what was wrong. Once again, I was left in that dark pocket of unknowing, where my shame sparked into fire. It took two years of trying to have sex, two years questioning the technicalities of virginity, and a series of Google searches to name the culprit.

Vaginismus is a disorder causing involuntary muscle contractions of the vagina. It can be generalized (happens all the time) or localized (just with that one guy). It can be moderate to severe. It can feel like a bouquet of dull, serrated knives opening inside of you. But it's always a good reason to use the square-peg, round-hole analogy. Mine is generalized, like my vagina has captured all my sexual repression, anxiety, and isolation. I am an inverted jar of dysfunction.

```
┌─────────────────────────────────────────────┐
│           FILE No. 8675309                    │
│              RAP SHEET                         │
│          Maryann Mental PD                     │
├───────────────────────────────────────────────┤
│ Name: Vaginismus                               │
├───────────────────────────────────────────────┤
│ Narrative: Vagina locks up like Pod Bay       │
│ doors when anything tries to enter.            │
├───────────────────────────────────────────────┤
│ Prior Charges:                                 │
├────────────────────────┬──────────────────────┤
│                        │ 2001, 2002,          │
│ Making it impossible to│ 2003, 2004,          │
│ use tampons            │ 2008, 2010,          │
│                        │ 2011, 2012           │
├────────────────────────┼──────────────────────┤
│ Frustrating sexual     │ 2013, 2014, 2016     │
│ encounters             │                      │
├────────────────────────┼──────────────────────┤
│ Fraud                  │ 2010, 2014           │
├────────────────────────┼──────────────────────┤
│ Fostering a sense of   │ 2013, 2014, 2016     │
│ complete defectiveness │                      │
└────────────────────────┴──────────────────────┘
```

Like passing my driver's test, sex was merely a matter of practice. The treatment plan I worked out from my WebMD research and a single book required a daily regimen of Kegels and dilators for what could be anywhere from two weeks to three months. Every day, I was supposed to clench my crotch and release 15 times. I convinced myself it was exciting to do this on my morning commute with a train full of strangers unaware of my super-human crotch strength. At home, I was supposed to practice my breathing and romance myself. I was supposed to imagine a place to relax, where I could exhale. My brain took me to a grocery store.

After days of breathing, just breathing, I started to work my way up to inserting the largest in a series of plastic penis-like objects in my vagina. I ordered a set of lavender dilators from Amazon and an electronic (*read*: secret) version of one of the three books that seems to exist on the subject. The pastel penis proxies arrived three days later along with two board games I'd ordered. The mailman left the package on my porch, and I remember worrying what someone would have thought had they stolen it. My shame was not derived from having an army of vibrators, it was that I'd ordered them with Bananagrams and Munchkin: Pirate's Booty.

Sometimes when I used them, I tried to set the mood. I would light candles, put on classical music, and touch myself, trying to elicit the same excitement that I felt when a man would touch me in the same way. But the element of (pleasant) surprise was missing. I once tried looking at photos of male celebrities. At a certain point, I gave up trying to use pseudo-pornography and started looking at pictures of cookies. My reaction to baked goods was essentially the same. Chris Hemsworth. Chocolate Chips. Whatever. Pictures had never worked for me. I had to fantasize romantic dinners, great seats to a show, and deep, intellectual conversation. Perhaps my aversion to porn was tied to my Guardian Period Angel and the silent necessity of porn to my childhood.

Quickly, the dilators became a matter of obligation. A matter of practice, a taker of my mental energy. Sex was supposed to be something you didn't have to work at. I'd failed my driving test once; I couldn't bomb something else fifteen-year-olds figure out every day. I was supposed to lie in bed with the cold plastic inside me for five then ten then fifteen minutes at a time each night. Fortunately, there was a *Law & Order* for almost every day of the week. I understand the irony of watching a show about sex crimes with a foreign object AirBnB-ing my vagina. But sex for me is work, even with toys. Maybe that's why I put it off until my twenties—I suffered from early-onset adulthood.

Two years of failure and a lack of knowledge had fueled the cycle. With each failure, I'd expect another. There I was, parallel parking a vibrator, learning just how to back in and cut the wheel. But I had only one voice to listen to. And, like any good puzzle, an instruction book.

**Bushwick
Brooklyn, NY
Even more years later**

In two weeks, I had gained enough control over my own body to comfortably insert even the laughably behemoth dilator. Not long after that, I got my license; I had real sex with a real person—without the tiny stabbing pains. I made the hole and peg the right fit. Although, it still takes finesse. My body spent all those years protecting me, driving away unwanted intruders. It's not so easy to reconcile—I often wonder which one of us betrayed the other. I still need the seatbelt, but at least I can unbuckle it when I stop moving. At least I can breathe.

Neon Disguises

Las Vegas: city of billboards, debauchery, and celebrity second chances; a desert oasis of burning lights and alcohol-fueled gambling binges. It's a city with an identity crisis: a metropolis among sand dunes, a tourist haven founded on poor imitations of the world's tourist havens. Casinos have no clocks or windows, as if the rules of time and space are inapplicable. The city's hotel carpets and gaudy stage productions flow so richly with hedonism that it invented a tagline to assert its lack of consequences for whatever occurs within its boundaries. It also invented the Drive-Thru wedding chapel. And it was the site of my first and last family vacation.

I was eight—the youngest, trailing behind by at least five years. It was my first plane ride, my first time in a hotel, my first excursion outside the vast borders of Montana. At the time, the Bozeman airport had only two gates—Delta and United—and the only nonstop flights went to Salt Lake City and Denver—hubs of Delta and United. We transferred in Salt Lake for what would have been a two-hour nonstop flight to Vegas. My brother Martin told me planes didn't crash much, except for the small two-row planes like the one we were boarding. Had my executive functioning skills been more developed, I might have quipped that if *I died, he would, too*. Instead, I turned to my mother for reassurance.

My parents told me I'd been on planes before but was too young to remember. We'd gone to Disney World when I was three. I assume I loved it, but not being able to know myself then, I can't say for sure. I enjoyed it when I was twelve and finally surpassed the yellow bar to ride roller coasters, but I was in Florida with only my mother. It was her mother's 70th birthday. I've never ridden a roller coaster with my siblings.

It was late afternoon when we arrived in the desert. There were two rows of slot machines in the lobby of The Excalibur hotel, which is what my parents deemed the most "family friendly" of the behemoths on the Las Vegas strip. I knew gambling was illegal at my age, which I assumed meant I could not be in the presence of gambling. While I waited for my parents, I glared at the machine, red cherries and green clovers and gold coins glaring back at me. I noticed a security guard, clad in non-threatening UPS brown with a badge and gadget-belt.

He made no effort to move.

I stared longer, a four-foot rebel testing the boundaries in a city where women adorn the sidewalks in rhinestone bikinis.

The guard did nothing.

Then my parents herded us to the room, and I trudged along, satisfied with my new status as a lawbreaker.

§

The Excalibur Hotel and Casino: an expansive tower of sleep/sex rooms capped with cartoon turrets—an almost-adequate replica of Cinderella's castle, but a castle, nonetheless. I remember the carpets: Hotel Carpet. I'd never stayed in a hotel before, but I recognized them instinctively. That beaten-down gaudiness; that imitation filigree stamped on dull primary colors; that overbearing effort to be distinctive.

Like every hotel on the Vegas Strip, The Excalibur came with its own C-list tourist experience and tacky restaurant. At The Excalibur, the two were folded into a single package: a medieval-themed dinner show. As much as I enjoyed fake kings making arbitrary decrees and watching horses run around inside, I was embarrassed to bang my fists on the table with the others in the amphitheater. I was embarrassed to eat with my hands. I didn't know how to bend such rules. Sure, I'd pulled a fast one on the casino guard, but this was *dinner.*

We visited all the major hotels on the Strip—except New York, New York, which was under construction. My glimpse of the half-built fake Statue of Liberty ignited something in me. I was disappointed to miss even the imitation of the city I would one day live in. But the hotels we did visit? They all had Hotel Carpet.

The Luxor was a hulking green glass pyramid with a basement museum of Egyptian things and Walkman audio tours. The Mirage was a bedazzled waterfall from the outside; inside, a bedazzled Siegfried and Roy made tigers disappear. We went to the restaurant. We didn't see the magicians with the tigers on our family vacation. Instead, I remember the tiny sharks in the lobby aquariums. I asked my brother if they were real sharks. Martin assured me they were. I didn't believe him, but it seemed equally unlikely that they were anything else. The Flamingo brought the Florida tropics to the Nevada desert. It was decorated like I imagined Ricky Ricardo's club would look in color. We ate at the restaurant there, too.

We drove past the Bellagio fountains and Greco-Roman gimmicks of Caesar's Palace. We toured the Hoover Dam and its drab industrial guts. We evaded poker tables everywhere, not speaking about the elephant and its circus in each room we wandered through, ignoring it like the velvet curtain that used to hang in Dad's video store. All their winding pathways of hotel carpet and cigarette smoke were like a maze keeping guests from too easily finding their way into the daylight. Each hotel was distinctively tacky and yet without any real identity. They began to swirl together into a sphere of lights. Everywhere, there were lights. I remember the lights. They were always on, blinking like defective stars: navigation guides for the drunk.

I liked the lights. But I was eight.

We visited Circus Circus, a pink circle in the sky containing an amusement park I was too small to enjoy. My brothers rode a roller coaster while I watched smaller children jolting back and forth on a plastic school bus. I was separated from the other children by a metal bar and from my family members by my age. My father came by, and I asked him if I could ride the school bus. It wasn't the roller coaster I wanted, but it was something.

My dad stood behind the metal bar and watched my dangling feet move up and down. It seemed slower there than it did from below. Looking down at my dad, it was lonely. But it was the closest I had to an adventure. While I drifted on a fake yellow school bus, my family wandered around a circle in the sky, as far from each other as we were from the ground below.

At the end of the week, we walked through a carnival on our way to some 3D film at the MGM Grand. There were bumper boats, child-sized and brightly colored. My forehead surpassed the yellow bar to ride them. I asked my parents if I could try, but there was no time. No time for my adventures.

§

That week in Las Vegas was our last family vacation, although we watched the film *Vegas Vacation* annually. My parents would go back once a year, staying just off the strip at a cheaper hotel with a nice buffet breakfast. They liked it there. They almost moved to Las Vegas in retirement, but Arizona was less expensive with the same booze-slathered atmosphere.

Like the shellac that coated Nevada's den of debauchery, our family's exterior hid our darker insides. After that trip, illness—diagnosed and undiagnosed—piled up in the passing years, like the Bellagio's stacks of poker chips. We hid beneath cartoon turrets and endless lights, suspended in windowless dissolution, distracting ourselves from the addictions and impulses harbored within our artificial borders. I remember the lights, blinking like defective stars. There was nothing real there. It was so easy to get lost.

Lunar Bodies

We were in a bad noir: two former lovers tilted toward one another in a dark speakeasy.

> *(a month earlier, on the cusp of*
> *the new year, I'd been startled*
> *half-awake*
> *by two brusque buzzes.)*

I hadn't heard from him in three months, but I'd spent the days before his text message churning mental drafts of how I could believably shroud an "I miss you" in a "Happy Holidays."

> *(my heart pumped in pace*
> *with each vibration, flooding*
> *me with uninvited*
> *self-awareness. I knew without looking*
> *that bright blip of green*
> *was his name—*
> *a little light in the dark.)*

Before I could find the courage—or perhaps lost what courage I'd held until then—I woke up on New Year's Eve to his "Happy Holidays." He hoped I was well.

But all I read was "I miss you."

A few weeks later, we sat in a tin-roofed bar drinking throat-stinging cocktails and saying everything other than what we wanted from each other.

I didn't ask if he still had a girlfriend. I didn't care. I felt entitled, however misguided that may have been. I wanted to tilt the universe in my favor, to disrupt the earth in some tiny way. He still didn't want to keep me—just to have me—

but we were magnets. It was up to gravity, to iron, to ions, to the moon. It was up to anything we could blame it on.

He asked me when I thought toilet paper was invented. He complained about *Playboy's* lackluster redesign and the reduced quality of its paper stock.

It was up to gravity. To the moon.

(I smiled in the dark.)

I woke up the next morning dripping in victory.

(truths often reveal themselves
in the dark.)

I didn't regret it. Or the months of clandestine sex that followed. I didn't regret when he left his girlfriend. I didn't regret that I wasn't his new one. And I didn't regret it when another year later he started seeing another someone else.

We became friends then, laid a layer between our magnets. I needed a friend— more than the moon—the moon we only know as it relates to ourselves—to Earth. It pulls the tides, as does the sun—three celestial objects in tension. Sometimes, Earth is at the center, sometimes the moon.

(I've been known to look at the ground and think about the stars.
sometimes forgetting my feet
are my only way to fly)

I needed a human to remind me how human I am. Flawed and lumpy and full of emotion. Rough, like the pages of *Playboy*.

After all, I can't control the moon.

Leviathan

Every forty seconds, somewhere in the world, someone takes their own life. As a collective, humanity cannot tolerate surviving another minute of existence. From the time I was about fifteen years old, I believed I would eventually die by suicide. It sounds bizarre, I know, to live a life assuming depression would one day claim me, like waiting to be hit by a bus. But I lived anyway. Suicide is an aspirational end for me; it's not outside my valence of possibility, but I probably won't ever follow through. Still, I like to know how I'd do it. I like to have an escape plan. I bought my first car after nine years living in New York City. I realized I was finally in possession of a practical method of killing myself.

An octopus is a living defense mechanism, built to ward off predators and protect its offspring. It can shoot ink to confuse attackers while it propels itself deeper into the ocean. But it will always return home; octopuses explore in circles, venturing away from their dens systematically.

Jumping off a bridge is too terrifying—the instinct for self-preservation would kick in. I suspect this would be the same with a gun or razorblades—too much time to reconsider. Hanging is too complicated without readily available rafters. Drano and antifreeze are easy enough to get, but painful on top of being slow and possibly ineffective. Pills always seemed the easiest method, but the margin of error is high. During the periods in my life when the possibility orbited closest, I wasn't taking medication, so it was never a viable option anyway. I never wanted to stick a friend or roommate with discovering my body either.

The best method available to me in recent years has been a train. But throwing myself in front of a subway car is also no guarantee. The New York City MTA posts signs in train cars with statistics: 172 people were hit by trains last year. Fifty died. I think they're trying to highlight the danger of leering over the platform or diving onto the tracks to retrieve expensive, pointless items, but I'm surprised by how many people survive. I can imagine my failed suicide attempt, becoming the asshole who held up the A train and living to see the shame through. I'd return to the existence I'd hated so much, having failed at the most serious commitment I'd made and probably having deformed myself in the attempt…

But now, I have a death machine. I can drive it off a bridge or mountain road, steal someone's garage and go peacefully in a cloud of carbon monoxide or take it into the woods and drive into a snowbank to freeze.

Driving again, after so long, I realized I had missed the way a steering wheel slips through my fingers, the smooth shushing sound it makes against my skin. I missed how driving takes every particle of concentration not to crash, how there is no leeway for my other anxieties to seep in. I missed the reminder that my hands are the only thing between my organs and the concrete walls of the RFK Bridge.

An octopus can spray ink to distract predators and inhibit sea creatures' senses of sight and smell. In lab experiments, octopuses have been known to squirt water at light bulbs and experimenters. Many octopuses simply don't perform the task expected of them. They understand captivity and usually rebel against it. Some have been known to jam their arms into water valves to raise the water level in their tank, flooding the lab in the process.

Taking your own life is a decision usually years in the making. It seeps into you every time depression hits, like ink stains on your bones. *What if? It'd be so easy…*

Depression robs your mind of the future. There is no possibility in captivity. What's the point of a life of probiotic yogurt and teeth-brushing and credit scores when all there is to look forward to is more credit scores and teeth-brushing and probiotic yogurt? Even if that captivity was forged in your own dark mind-matter, even if you *know* that captivity is only imagined, it's captivity nonetheless. And the only way to free yourself from the imagined chains is to shut off the mind that makes them. Suicide may be the wrong solution, but it's a solution.

What I should be doing is confronting the monster. Instead, I try to outrun it. The anxiety helps. Anxiety obscures sadness, muddying it with immediacies. It's a schedule of worries flashing in my cerebral cortex, prodding at me to *go go go. Get out of bed. Move. Shower. Exist.*

I fill my days with work, where I lacquer on a smile and keep the endless reel of self-hate at bay by expelling my fears through tapping fingers on a keyboard or finding friends to drink with during the hours I know I won't be able to sleep. I watch television, occasionally read a book—when I can quiet my own narration enough to retain words—to observe a world in which I don't have to live. I write when I have to. When I can't keep up with my anxiety's expectations. When the water level floods.

Octopus arms are semi-autonomous. They can regrow lost tentacles. Their bodies are covered in neurons, lending them a similar intellectual capacity to vertebrates than their closer invertebrate relatives. Though a central brain controls most of their actions, octopuses' complex body parts often ad-lib based on what they sense around them. As predator and prey, the octopus relies on its complex body to survive. In addition to crushing tensile strength, many species have venomous bites to paralyze prey.

The crystal-blue reality is that the world isn't fair. We don't always get what we deserve. Depressed people understand this. Their bodies are imbued with it. Psychologist Martin Seligman called it *learned helplessness*: enough failures remove all desire to keep trying. Some people can handle setback after setback because they can blame the weather, or the world. But those with depression have a pessimistic attributional style. We believe every failure is a personal failure; each one is internal (my fault), global (*every* mistake is my fault), and stable (they will *always* be my fault). That's when I feel most myself: when the sea inside me is calm. When the mundane worries vanish and my dark reality surfaces. When I'm no longer trying to help myself. Yet those are the times when I struggle to put pants on, one leg at a time or not. My body becomes paralyzed, like I was hit with a lightning bolt of sadness.

For me, depression is when I drop a dish and watch it crack and remember that I'm broken, too. It's when I order chicken fingers for takeout and they forget all the dipping sauces and I'm so sad I'm missing the best part, but I think I probably don't deserve dipping sauce anyway. I'll cry a puddle onto the kitchen floor and from it summon a dark leviathan. I cannot function when I am myself.

Sometimes, it feels like I'm hallucinating while watching myself hallucinate—like I'm standing in a corner, trying to tell myself the sea monster circling me is just that, a myth. I *know* I am not hated, not completely alone, not completely worthless. But knowing has never been a prerequisite for believing. It is my fault. It is always my fault. It will always be my fault.

Of course, my brain orchestra returns, my anxiety regrows me. The leviathan swims away, and my mind invents new distractions: a new dress, a creative project, a frantic scramble for a promotion.

Though I can't see a future—any future—some part of me keeps fighting for it. The part that needs to be liked, that needs not to fail. The part I wish would release me into the deep. The part that hasn't learned helplessness yet. Or maybe, that part just likes probiotic yogurt.

An octopus can change color to camouflage itself. Octopus skin contains photoreceptors that detect the environment around them, allowing the animal to blend into the sea floor. The closely related cuttlefish frequently changes color in response to perceived attackers. Sometimes, they change colors—bright shades of red and orange and yellow—for what appears to be no reason at all.

Like the immaculate house I grew up in, my amiable sheen and outgoing gloss deflect suspicion. It only takes a coat of lipstick and a dab of concealer to hide a bruise. I learned by watching my mother. I learned to feign authenticity, to fit in from the outside. But I am a shy person who learned to wear bright shades of pink and yellow to hide my internal black and grey. I am a depressed person trapped in a happy one. Sometimes I think I am the opposite of a pod person.

I was in therapy for three years. Two, then three times a week. My therapist would always ask me about my feelings, but I couldn't wade beneath the anxiety to find the answer. We'd brought up medication as a possibility early on, but I never followed through. The anxiety seemed to be working then. Eventually, my superhuman workload outswam me. And the black seeped through.

"I know you made an appointment, but the psychiatrist wasn't available for over a month from now," she said. "You said yesterday you didn't feel like it was urgent. Are you feeling differently today?"

I didn't want to worry her. But I didn't have a smile left in me. "Honestly?" I said, "I don't have faith anything will work, so I'm not sure it matters when I go."

"That's really important. I'm glad you said that."

"I mean…it's been a long time since I was on medication. Maybe if it's for the anxiety, it'll be different. But the anxiety is also what keeps me from…giving up."

"It keeps you living."

"Yeah."

"This is the most I've ever felt you talking about your feelings. Like this is really you, living under the surface."

I nodded. "I'm definitely more myself when I'm like this." I paused. "But I also can't function like this."

"How does it feel to talk about it?"

I searched for an emotion, trying to pay attention to my hands, my feet, to analyze and process. I tried to formulate a correct answer, something true, but perhaps insincere. Instead, something else rolled out:

"Honest."

Because it lacks bones, an octopus can flatten itself, fitting into cracks to hide and lay eggs in. While defending their eggs, octopuses sometimes forget to feed themselves. Most species live only two to four years, yet they continue to reproduce, living just long enough to make more octopuses. More octopuses that will live for two to four years, living just long enough to make more octopuses.

When the anxiety evaporates, it's like I can see the world with total clarity. Total probiotic clarity. I understand how little it all matters and ask what the hell I'm doing. The depression surfaces again and again, reminding me I am flawed, *again*. It oozes like ink. It stains me.

Although I never attempted suicide, I've come close, but something has always pulled me back. Tiny things: my cat, a text from a friend, the thought of making my roommate find my body. When I was closest, enveloped in my own dark—once, alone on a hotel room floor; once, crying on my own foam mattress—I thought of razorblades.

It wasn't the method I expected to choose.

Suspended in nighttime, wishing for the safety of sleep, I saw flashes of blood, slices of flesh erupting in red. The images of opening myself were beautiful and freeing. As I convulsed in tears, Marzipan's rubber paws pressed on my back like stamps marked URGENT.

I cried myself paralyzed. My body ad-libbing, refusing to listen to my complex brain. I cried new lines into my face one night. Not even makeup covered them. I was out in the light, above the water.

§

While making a sandwich one day, a couple of years into my meds, I realized I hadn't neared the line in almost three years. *I'm here*, I thought. *I'm here. I'm in this life. For good.* I had made so many sandwiches, merely to move the hands of the clock that ticks away my existence. Suddenly, there were many more sandwiches to make, not the sandwiches of an indefinite death march, but sandwiches for the sake of sandwiches.

So many with depression wilt, and droop, below the threshold—that thin barrier between seeing trying as possible and succumbing to the ease of giving up. Depression is isolating and self-fueling: the more alone you feel, the more alone you become. The barrier is most often impermeable; once you sink, you drown. When you've spent so long hiding your depression, the smallest crack will reveal you. Like most monsters, it doesn't like the light. Talking about it helps. Three years in therapy and several months on the right medication were enough to lock the escape hatch. As much as I want to take a battering ram to it, I can't. I'm stuck in my tank, with no light bulbs to squirt or filters to block. I can't move backward anymore—as much as I still don't want to move forward. Here I am, wearing yellow in the yogurt aisle, wishing I could be an octopus, living only two to four years. Here I am, driving over a commuter bridge with an unbreakable concrete barrier, heading toward some other side I can't see, and yet I know I'll get there. Here I am, unchained and emerged from the deep.

worry, the panic, the hurry hurry hurry that shocks me out of bed. And It is the thing that tentacles to crush prey and rip it apart. But an octopus and the depression ~~grab~~ Suctions my morsels, it gets

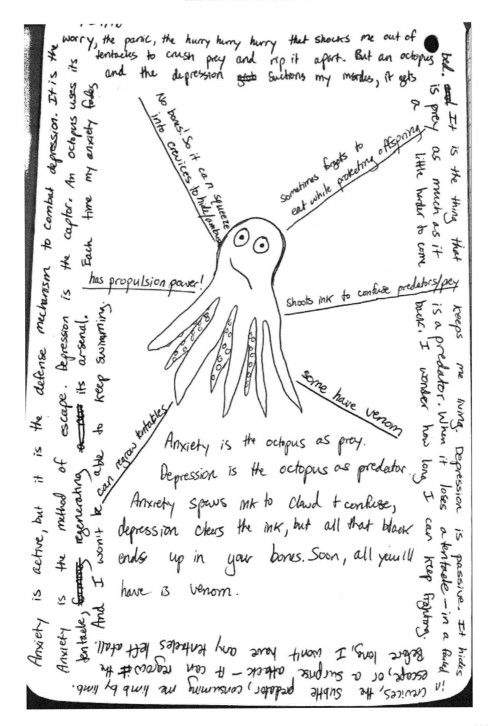

No bones! So it can squeeze into crevices to hide/ambush

Sometimes forgets to eat while protecting offspring

has propulsion power!

Shoots ink to confuse predators/prey

some have venom

can regrow tentacles

is prey as much as it is a predator. An octopus uses its little harder to come. Each time my anxiety fades

It is the thing that keeps me living. Depression is passive. It hides in is a predator. When it loses a tentacle — in a failed escape, or a surprise attack — it can regrow# the back, I wonder how long I can keep fighting.

Anxiety is the octopus as prey.

Depression is the octopus as predator.

Anxiety spews ink to cloud + confuse, depression clears the ink, but all that black ends up in your bones. Soon, all you'll have is venom.

Anxiety is active, but it is the defense mechanism to combat depression. It is the method of escape. Depression is the captor. Depression is the arsenal.

Anxiety is the tentacle, ~~forever~~ regenerating, able to keep swimming. And I won't be able to regrow tentacles

Before long, I won't have any tentacles left at all. In crevices, the subtle predator, consuming me limb by limb.

Supernova

My mother does not steal the spotlight; she is the spotlight. She is the thing that can make you seen and unseen in an instant. And there's no better spectacle of her narcissism than shopping with her.

When I was a teenager, our excursions typically involved her deciding what parts of my body I should hide; sometimes, they'd involve her buying a pile of clothes that showed off whatever parts of her body she wanted. From middle school onward, any interactions between my mother, myself, and my clothes orbited my breasts. They were the planets around which Mom's criticisms swirled. If something was wrong with my outfit, my boobs were at fault.

"There's a lot of cleavage." She'd say. Always frowning. Like my bust line was an under-seasoned entrée.

Then, she'd adjust the neckline of the dress I was trying on and shake her head.

"It's very revealing."

I'd turn to the mirror and stare at myself, wondering if my cleavage was as grotesque as she made it out to be. By 16, my breasts had grown too large for the bras we could find in the mall, but nothing made them feel more monstrous than my mother's unwavering infatuation with them. I remember so many weekend afternoons in fluorescent dressing rooms, just staring into the mirror, silently asking *what is so wrong with my body?* I'd see my stolid face reflected back at us. Then just at me—my mother would walk away, searching for something she was going to like better. And I would be left alone, staring at myself.

§

This is the kind of story I'd want to share in my mother's eulogy. It would be a fitting tribute: a revealing anecdote that is more about myself than about her. Funerals are for the stories we most remember about those we've lost, to resurrect them briefly as we ease into the reality of their nonexistence. They are rarely a time for honesty.

§

"My mother was always after something better. And usually, she got it. [1] She was effervescent. A truly memorable personality. And her absence is a great loss to the countless people whose lives she touched.[2] Mom felt things deeply. It was one of so many things that made her unique.[3] She had an ability to connect with strangers. I remember her once talking to our waiter and learning that he was a firefighter, waiting tables until his back healed. He'd been in a motorcycle accident. She asked and, in return, he had started telling her things that might matter one day, things that might be nice to say at someone's funeral."

Pause for reflection.

---

[1] Mom will share almost anything with a stranger, from the news that both of her daughters failed their first driver's tests to the details of her own recent colonoscopy. She's made a habit of ranting at wait staff, holding them uncomfortably long at our dining table. When a server stops by to ask if she wants a refill of wine—she always does—my mother's histrionic tentacles grab hold and our wait staff are submerged in her emotional ocean, like a lost breadcrumb sloshing in her wine glass.

[2] Usually, the conversation begins with something like the weather and grows into a life story of the oldest sibling at the table. *Arthur is recovering from cancer*, she'd brag. Suffering was always an achievement.

[3] I first visited my parents in their retirement while I was on a winter break from college. It was the first I'd seen them in almost a year. They took me to the Olive Garden, and my mother opened her act by telling our waiter that he looked like Harry Potter.

When she asked his name, he said, "I'm Josh."

Then, she reached up to his chest, where his name tag dangled backwards, and turned it around like a butterfly in the palm of her hand. She read his name out loud: Josh. She looked to my father and I for confirmation.

His name was definitely Josh.

The Olive Garden isn't particularly crowded at 3:00 p.m. on a Tuesday, so Josh was content to humor my mother. She went through her typical topics: the weather is nice today, we make margaritas every Thursday, my husband plays a lot of golf. Then she began asking questions.

"My father's best friend had died six months earlier in a motorcycle crash. As it turned out, our waiter's mother died in a crash a few years before. I think, in that moment, we all felt the same bittersweet sadness of memory mixed with loss.[4]"

Beat.

"Thanks to my mom."

"I'm sure that's a feeling we are all familiar with today."

Hold for audience reflection. Then cry to yourself. You're the only one listening anyway.

"She can go on forever about nothing…"

Hold for audience chuckle.

"…and still learn something that might be nice to share in a stranger's eulogy."

Stop crying.

"Her outgoing nature was certainly her greatest asset. We can all agree she had a…big personality. But that was just Mom.[5]"

---

[4] It's humbling to share a deep emotion with a stranger. On one hand, it's a comforting reminder that you're never entirely alone; on the other, it's the disappointing reality that you aren't unique. Despite her empathy for strangers, my mother has a way of making me feel both unexceptional and alone.

[5] After a moment of mutual despair, we all forced smiles, and Josh left and returned with our food. My mom went into her next line of questioning. She asked how old he was and, without waiting for an answer, told him that I was single, 19, and going to college in New York. Ignoring the logistical impracticality of our situation—and the obvious humiliation splattered on my face—Mom plowed ahead trying to arrange a relationship between our waiter and me.

I think we're past the crying phase now.

"She will be missed. But her time on earth has made an impression on everyone in this room."

Long beat.

"I'll never forget her enthusiasm. For everything.[6]"

He asked if my mother wanted more wine—she did—and went off to do her bidding. My mom quickly alleviated the silence in his absence, talking about neighbors and wine and Arizona. Each word pushed me deeper into the corner of our booth, compressing me back into a square of shame. When our heroic bearer of booze returned, my mother put forth her glass, loaded with new questions for him. New facts for his eulogy, new ammunition for companionship.

I sat in the corner, sharing the same pleather-coated seat as my mother without any words passing between us. Like her wine glass, she'd offered me up in exchange for admiration and made the kind of connection with a stranger she struggled to find with me.

[6] I looked forward to my junior prom for months after I found out it was on my 17th birthday. I didn't expect a date, nor did I get one, but I had hoped for a gown. Special occasions have always most appealed to me as an excuse to dress up.

My mother initially suggested I wear an old homecoming dress, none of which were up to the Audrey Hepburn standards I had hoped for. But while bartering over eggs and getting directions to the town square in French class, we managed to squeeze in a half-English discussion of Prom—which incidentally is derived from French—and *les robes*. My generous senior friend offered me one of her dresses on loan. That weekend, I drove to her house, which sat atop its own hill, and she opened her closet to me.

Half a dozen gowns dangled from cloth-covered hangers. I felt like a kid seeing a magician for the first time. I wore a stupid grin on my face and everything.
My friend had three dresses I liked. She let me borrow all of them. I draped them over the back seat of the car, smoothing the fabric with my fingers, and sped off into the distance with my bounty.

Get lost in your imagination, briefly.

"For my junior prom, I had hoped for an expensive, extravagant dress. But my mother, understandably, didn't want to drop $300 on something I'd wear once and not even get married in. I was going to borrow a dress from a friend, but on the morning of the dance, my mom leapt into action.[7] With six hours until I had to meet my friends, my mother ushered me into the minivan and we drove to ROSS. Mom and I dug through leftovers of leftovers as I counted the minutes until my high school's junior and senior classes would be bumping and grinding on a linoleum floor. My graduating class, by the way, was singled-out in state and national news for Mormon backlash against the dirty dancing at our prom. But I got my movie montage: a flurry of colors flying from shopping racks, heaps of dresses on the fitting room floor, stuck zippers, poofy sleeves, tears, head shakes, thumbs up and down, and top 40 hits from four years ago streaming above us."

"We found a dress, miraculously, on the same day as my prom.[8] And I have this

---

[7] After going full rom-com in all my friend's gowns—trying each on and giggling to myself in the mirror—

Get lost in your imagination again. But even more briefly.

I settled on a long off-white gown dotted with glittering pink roses. It was strapless and flowing and a mature degree of sparkly: the prom dress of my dreams.

The morning of the dance—the morning of my 17th birthday—I descended the stairs, envisioning myself in *Roman Holiday,* or *Sabrina,* considering which of my shoes were most fitting for a princess. I showed my mother the dress and, at the sight of her face, my heart shrank.

"You don't like it?"

"It's just…not you."

This was news to me.

"And it doesn't really fit…here," she gesticulated toward some part of my body. "It doesn't look good. Why don't we get you something else?"

[8] We found the dress that my mother deemed the most "me." It was turquoise. Covered in glitter. Floor-length. Halter-top. It was fun. It was juvenile. It was not Audrey Hepburn. Come to think of it, it oozed cleavage. And I had to tie the halter top so tightly to support my breasts that it hurt my neck.

crazy memory—the best kind of crazy, of course—of me and my mom.[9] She was spontaneous. Once, we wandered into a shoe store amidst our errands and I pulled this pair of stilettos out of the sale rack, intrigued by the tiny shoelaces on the toes. She bought them for me because they were on sale. And they were Carlos Santana shoes (we didn't know he made shoes). And because they were the last pair.[10] She didn't want to miss an opportunity."

Another long beat.

Perhaps if I'd had enough bourbon, I'd say out loud what I really wanted to. I'd describe the times we would go shopping and I'd find a nicely tailored button down that needed only a safety pin at the bust to keep from popping open. My mother would frown and toss her head side to side in disgust. We'd go shopping for something specific and leave with nothing, or we'd go out for dish soap and return with an armful of V-neck t-shirts. She learned that large-chested women should wear V-necks, according to television makeover shows, so I owned a drawer of them. Somehow, I attended public school, but seemed to have a uniform. As an adult, I've discovered a trove of other shapes and cuts I can drape over my boobs with some success.

---

[9] Shopping with Mom yielded sporadic treasures. Such random reinforcement is the best way to get someone to repeat a behavior. Generally, trying to apply scientific concepts to my mother's behavior is like walking into a labyrinth. I can, however, explain my own unwinnable desire to believe she loved me. Not for her to love me. Just for me to believe it.

In psychology, reinforcement refers to a response to a behavior that's meant to influence future behavior. B.F. Skinner was a pioneer of behavioral psychology, training pigeons with food pellets in his lab. In one experiment, he had pigeons push levers to receive food. Some got the food after a minute passed. Some, after they pushed the lever four times. Some, at random. The last group pushed the lever most often. They didn't want to miss their opportunity.

While my mom was buying perfume at Macy's once, I tried on a jacket to entertain myself. When she saw me in it, she screamed in glee and insisted she buy it for me. She bought me a pair of four-inch patent-leather stilettos in much the same way.

[10] It didn't matter that I was in high school and had nowhere to wear them.

Maybe the liquor would kick in and I'd say,

"My mother tended to fixate, as all her children do. She'd find one article of clothing that worked and buy twenty of them, in every color, or she'd take up a hobby and suddenly our living room was full of knitted mittens, or we'd eat chicken-cordon-bleu and lamb shanks every week to the sounds of her complimenting herself."

Pause to take in what you're saying. Follow the alcohol's instincts. It's what she would do.

"I always found it strange that a woman raising one daughter with an eating disorder would be such a perfectionist with her other daughter's clothes. When our opinions on an item differed, mine was vetoed. She loved me in this and hated me in that. She was rarely indifferent. This translated to: Mom loves me or Mom hates me. Imperfect is wrong. In my mid-twenties, I bought a dress I found while killing time at the Gap. The middle was slightly too big, like the end of a finger in a glove. But otherwise, perfect. I purchased it despite my mother's soundtrack running ear to ear. *It bunches,* she would say. I felt her *tsk tsk tsk* reverberating off the dressing room walls. In a tiny act of defiance, I wore it on Thanksgiving while visiting my parents in Arizona. She gave me the same look as when she'd seen me in that jacket years earlier: Love."

Take a deep breath.

"Not a word about the imperfect crinkle across the middle. The next day we set out shopping. Fixated on that perfect-but-imperfect dress, my mother couldn't find anything she thought worth buying for me. She returned home with $300 of new clothes for herself. I, having inadvertently outdone myself, went back with nothing. My mother has a way of making me feel both unexceptional and alone. I'd finally been bold enough to do something I loved despite her, and to ignore the dissatisfaction she engrained in me. I'd gotten her approval, and still she fixated on what was flawed. She was always seeking something better. It was me who never got it."

Throw back the last of the bourbon.

"And she isn't even really dead yet... Once, I'd snatched a bit of happiness for myself—happiness in imperfection—and she stole it back from me. As I stand here, delivering a hypothetical eulogy, ambivalent about what is right or wrong to say, I am realizing that it's only fitting to steal it back."

North Star

The phone rings. It's my sister. We haven't talked in three months.

I pause whatever I'm watching on Netflix and answer.

"Hey! How are you? It's been a while."

I put my sister on speaker and rest the phone on my desk. She's in Arizona now, almost 40, living a few towns away from our parents. I'm alone, just shy of 30, in New York. "Yeah. I know. I'm good. It's— How are you?"

"Good."

I contemplate pizza toppings from Domino's in the pause.

"How's Rick?" I ask. "And the baby?"

"They're good…she cries a lot."

"Yeah. I mean…babies." I opt for pineapple.

"I know. I just never sleep."

"I think Mom said Arthur used to cry all the time."

"Ugh, Mom."

I choose pepperoni instead. "What did she do now?"

"She just…she always complains."

"Well, at least you have her and Dad nearby. That must be a big help." I realize I can order different toppings on each half of my pizza.

"Yeah," she sighs. "But I have to deal with mom." She's making a joke. I think.

"Heh. Yeah…" I want to add chicken wings. Neither of us speak while I make my decision. I look at the phone. She's still there.

"How's the, uh, new house?"

"Good. We're still unpacking. Didn't you move?"

"Yeah. I have a fireplace that doesn't work."

She laughs. "That's helpful."

"Well now it's just a really ornate and poorly situated shelf that I can't put anything underneath."

We laugh at my poor fireplace's expense.

I place my order. The Domino's Pizza Tracker tells me Armand is making my pizza. I look at the phone. Still there.

"I…"

"Did you know Mom is teaching eight water aerobics classes?" my sister says. "She won't shut up about it."

"Sounds like Mom." Armand has put my pizza in the oven. "You know she couldn't be bothered to teach me to tie my shoes, but she loves teaching water aerobics."

We laugh together, thousands of miles apart.

"Who taught you to tie your shoes?"

"You did."

"Oh! Right."

"Well…" I say, "I have to make some dinner. I don't want to keep you— it's nice to hear from you."

"Yeah! Love you."

I un-pause my movie. "Love you, too. Talk soon."

§

One of my last clear memories of my sister before she was sick was when she taught me to tie my shoes. While my kindergarten classmates made their way to our elementary school gym for our first day of P.E. class, my teacher made me stay back in the classroom—alone—until I could lace my sneakers. Velcro had apparently gone out of fashion with my fifth birthday, but I hadn't learned how to tie the knots to accompany my new sneakers. Squatting on a foam mat in front of my cubby hole, I wrapped my shoelaces together and tucked them under the tongue as I wiped snotty tears from my face with the crook of my elbow. I wandered the hallway, alone, and had to take my spot at the front of the gym, late and ashamed. At home, I went to my sister for solace.

"You take this one and make a loop," she said, pinching my hot pink shoelaces, the perfect accessories for my light pink sneakers. "Then take this one and you pull it through, like this." Her long and nimble fingers wrapped the laces and twisted them into a tidy bow.

"I don't…get it."

She showed me again.

"I…can't," I said as I fumbled the sad little strings.

She thought for a moment, recalibrating to the needs of a five-year-old. "Here," she said, folding each lace into a loop. "You can also do it like this." She swooped them together: Bunny ear. Bunny ear. Knot.

"I think I get it." I folded one loop, then another. Slowly, I wrapped one around the other and pulled them taut. They flopped onto my shoes, two limp pink ovals clinging together.

"You did it!"

I smiled. It would take me a full minute, but I could tie my shoes. My sister showed me the intricacies of knots. Perhaps she knew then how likely I was to unravel; she even taught me to double-knot them. And with a final tug of the bow, my shame subsided.

These gentle moments began to disappear as my sister's anorexia replaced me as the newest addition to our family. Her time was spent fighting an illness she appeared to have chosen. But my sister is more than her eating disorder. I often forget this. She is a mother now, a wife, an artist. For many years, she was my north star. She was a constant of wisdom—keeper of the knowledge of shoe-tying, baking, ice skating, and scrapbooking—but also a permanent trauma.

The most visceral pain is in the images I remember. How thin she was. How impossibly frail. A decade of starvation ravaged her body. I used to have flashbacks of her wrists moments before they were tucked back beneath a sleeve, or of the white of her face, pale as a ghost.

The most enduring pain is in what I cannot remember. As we got older, she grew thinner and more reclusive. Our relationship was already cleaved by our seven-year age gap, adding my sister's increasing physical and mental absence left a gaping fissure between us. The few childhood memories I do have of her feel as if they've been pasted over with vellum; what remains is a general unhappiness I directed toward her. I remember that we played with a Ouija Board sometimes, and that she would scold me for touching fragile figurines in Hallmark. I remember that she dropped out of school and spent days at home doing crossword puzzles and eating meals with our mother. I wish I could dig into the tiny, intimate moments that sisters share and reveal something beautiful. But our relationship is made more of what I do not remember than what I do.

§

I do remember that my sister had a pair of cartoonish pig earrings. Their rosy piglet faces would bounce alongside her own on the few occasions she wore them. I was always surprised she'd be willing to wear anything that invited even a remote comparison between herself and a symbol of gluttony. Every time I'd see them, smiling at me as they dangled on her tidy jewelry display, I felt a twinge of envy as I anticipated the day when I could wear them. She wouldn't let me wear them, even when I had my ears pierced. I never even liked pigs, but I wanted the earrings. It was probably because she wouldn't let me have them that I wanted them so much. When I was a teenager, she gave them to me unceremoniously when she moved out. They're still tucked away in my jewelry box, having made it through half a dozen apartments. I wear jewelry nearly every day and my wardrobe drips with whimsy, yet I almost never wear the pig earrings.

§

Andromeda started quilting shortly after she was diagnosed with anorexia. She'd quit dancing and needed to replace the fixation. My mother had taught us both to sew, but I lacked my sister's dedication, and nimble fingers. The carefully formed lines of Andromeda's arabesques and relevés translated easily into the winding threads of embroidery. She stitched quilts too intricate for my tiny, shaky hands. I could trace patterns in them with my fingers, like dot-to-dots, imagining the lines of the Little Dipper in the threads. When I went away to college, about a year after her recovery, Andromeda gave me a quilt. It was meant to be decorative—not for warmth—impractical for a dorm room made of 70 percent bed. The quilt was full of blues and purples, like a geometric sky. The back was a print of infinite penguins. They were my favorite animal at the time, but I choose not to read into them being flightless birds. I had nowhere to put it except my bed, so I draped it over the end of my dorm mattress. It didn't belong—in that room or in my possession. Embroidered in a corner, my sister had written: *To Maryann, My sister, my best friend, my guardian angel. Love, Andromeda.*

I've kept the quilt but have always been unsure what to do with it. It carries such weight; it frightens me. It took me almost fifteen years of owning these things to realize: she passed on objects in place of conversation, emotion, and empathy. Her life existed within our house, within her bedroom. My sister and I did not talk about our latest crushes. She didn't have any. We didn't commiserate about our homework. She didn't have any. We didn't bond over movies I rented from our dad's video store. She didn't watch any. Even watching my brother play video games felt in some way like sharing. Martin and I would talk and joke as he played *Grand Theft Auto,* honoring the ancient rite of passage for older siblings to clandestinely want to show off their video game prowess to younger siblings, and for the younger siblings, for some inexplicable reason, to be excited to watch. It's a bond formed from the deadlock between forging self-identity and wanting to emulate those you admire. I wanted what my sister wanted, and I spent my time as she spent hers: alone.

§

Andromeda danced ballet for more than 10 years. I tried ballet for about three months, when I was six, and quit because practicing was hard, and I saw no reward in it. (I would also speculate that I wasn't very good—my favorite part of dance class was the warmup, where I could pretend to be a unicorn and skip around the dance studio.) Andromeda had a friend who frequently won state-wide dance contests and I asked my mother why my sister never won. Of course, I viewed my older siblings with god-like talent because I had no frame of reference, but my sister really was an excellent ballerina. This isn't something I remember well; it's something I know from many others. Her dance teachers, my mother, her friends, my friends who danced at the same studio. Her work ethic outmatched her talent tenfold. My sister is determined and obsessive in the pursuits she chooses, including her eating disorder. She could have had a successful career as a dancer, had she wanted to. So why didn't she win Montana Sweetheart Dance 1997? She didn't enter the competition, or any others.

I began to understand the structure of competition—you must enter one to win one, no one is plucked from the ether—but I couldn't understand why my sister continued dancing if not to win. What was it in me that needed a glittering trophy and in her that didn't? What was it in her that she could be so ordered, so disciplined, for no tangible reward?

Maybe this is why she was anorexic and I wasn't. Andromeda needed to shape her existence into neat bows and intricate threads; it was the process that mattered to her. I quit dancing, and sewing, and most other pursuits without quick reward. She was the kind to construct a map, regardless of where she was going. I was the kind to follow the stars, which often started with following her.

§

I was six when my sister showed me how to color. I had four coloring books fanned across the kitchen table and a gallon Ziploc full of battle-worn crayons spilling in front of me. She asked to color a page, which I saw as an invasion. I searched for the least interesting scene in my *Rugrats* book.

"You can color this one," I said, and shoved a coloring book to her.

I observed her fingers as they worked their way around the shape of a character's dress; she colored in crisp, delicate lines. I put my crayon down.

"How do you do that?"

"I just trace around the line and color inside that. Here." She showed me how she created a line abutting the pre-drawn boundary, doubling the margin of error for her to color within.

With a brown crayon, I traced the outline of a rabbit. My tongue squeezed its way out the side of my mouth in concentration. I was proud of this, until I made it to step two. My margins weren't wide enough, and my page became the same kind of mess as always. My sister's was flawless, like her bedroom and her ballet routines. Then I realized what she'd done.

"Angelica isn't blue! Her dress is supposed to be purple," I said.

"Well, you can color her whatever colors you want."

"But on the show, her dress is purple."

She'd ruined my coloring book, tainting reality with her lines, her delicacy, her creativity. I was envious. I wanted to emulate her, to feel even half as perfect as she seemed to be. I never asked her about her eating disorder, the *how*, the *why*, the *what's wrong with you*. I was afraid, and I didn't know how to ask. We lived in the same house for 13 years, at least seven of which I mostly remember, yet I struggle to recall any conversation we had after I turned ten. It's illogical—my memory must be defective. She taught me to tie my shoes and how to color, she was my guide, my oracle of sisterly knowledge. But Andromeda got sick when I was a child and she moved out when I was 13. And she was gone long before that. Even though I don't remember it, my sister showed me how to disappear.

§

Just before she eventually entered her last treatment center, Andromeda ran away. She came to visit and stayed overnight, but she absconded from the house in the middle of the night, having promised she would go to a rehab center the next day. I wrote her an angry letter in my creative writing class that morning. I still have the journal it's written in, from my junior year of high school. Just like the quilt and the earrings: I've kept it because I wasn't sure if I could throw it out. It's good that I didn't, because now I know the letter basically says, "Fuck you, I hate you," in about 30 teenager-y ways. It was the kind of exercise you were supposed to write for catharsis—to put it in an envelope, address it, and burn it or something. I never did burn it, obviously, but I never showed it to her either. That was our relationship: endless, un-mailed, possibly charred letters to each other. Though I doubt hers had many *fuck yous* considering the guardian angel quilt. This is all I have, objects passed between us like stardust. My physical mementos of my sister are these: kind words from her to me; my angry words about her; a pair of pig earrings.

§

A few years ago, my mother found what she thought was a dead rabbit underneath a bush in her yard, and called me about it, concerned. When it migrated to her patio, she realized it was playing dead. Soon, a second rabbit joined it. She sent me a photo: two limp rabbits splayed in the Arizona sun, falsely calm in their feigned deaths. They occupied the same three-square feet of space in complete detachment. One must have signaled the other, calling her forth to live in faux death together. Andromeda and I have April birthdays, which meant a lot of bunny-themed gifts. I'm sure the intention behind what became a small stuffed bunny army was one of convenience and cuteness, but rabbits spend their lives outrunning death, playing dead, and dying. They *survive*. My sister and I learned to survive in much the same way, constantly outrunning our own demise.

Andromeda was as unimaginably thin as she was committed to her illness, but she recovered eventually. It took forcing her into treatment, which I would normally strongly advise against, but somehow, she survived. I imagine it was the same drive that made her such a vigilant anorexic that also saved her life. She was unwavering in her commitments, be it ballet, quilting, or starvation. She was obsessive; constant.

I never expected her to live, and the narrative I wove from that assumption left a wound of my own creation. I disengaged from sisterdom early on, afraid that "sister" could be a temporary post. I did my best to detach completely, not that there was much to detach from. She spent her days in her room or her sewing studio. She didn't let me into the corners of her world, and I didn't knock at their doors. The best way to avoid something is to know exactly where it is. My sister became the central point of my detachment, like the North Star on a winter night reminding me of the ice that waits below.

§

Plunkett was a stuffed cow, and companion to our many bunnies. Plunkett spent each day propped on the pillows of Andromeda's made-to-hotel-regulations bed. She named him Plunkett because he made a "moo" sound when you turned him upside down (or "plunked" him). Plunkett was black and white with a black buzz cut, two yellow horns, and no cow spots. We had not yet learned, or perhaps simply didn't care, that cows are female. My sister showed me how to shake him back and forth to distort the sound and we'd laugh at poor Plunkett's expense.

We often bonded over cruelty to others, making fun of weird people at the mall, inventing sad life stories for poorly dressed women, or complaining about our mother. Faced with the threat of implosion from our own introspection, we turned our self-judgements to the world around us. Because my sister and I have rarely been able to talk to each other about each other.

§

At her wedding, my sister danced with her husband to John Legend's "All of Me." She was 32—eight years into her recovery, which was almost as long as she'd been anorexic.

Martin was standing next to me as we watched. He leaned over to say, "I never thought she'd be around for this, you know?"

"I know," I said, and I started crying. I was a spigot of emotional repression. I cried every tear I withheld for the nine years she was sick. I cried because she was happy. I cried because I was not. I cried because I couldn't stop. I was crying because it was expected of me. Years of rage and sadness and uncertainty flooded the fortifications I'd erected over a decade, and I cried. Vehemently. My whole body jiggled. I cried because of every feeling I have never been able to tell my sister. I cried every feeling I'd never been able to have. I thought that might have done it, loosened the cap of whatever unrealized rage bubbled inside me. Maybe it was healing. Maybe it was letting go. It was a flourish of anger and memory crushed swiftly by reality: how do we begin to make up for 30 years of silence?

Growing up, I imagined…Maybe we can cherish the objects passed between us as the totems of love they are. Maybe we can write about rabbits as metaphor. Maybe we can wish on shooting stars. Maybe all we can do is laugh together, thousands of miles apart and say *I love you, talk soon.*

Dusk

New York City winters sting. Skyscrapers darken the sidewalks, which are dusted with white salt to melt the black ice underneath. Gray gives way to gray. The lights from overcrowded apartment buildings make the stars imperceptible, especially in watery winters. Snow falls and melts, trodden by boots and taxi tires. Slush coats the concrete and leaks back into the wind-whipped water. Temperatures plunge in early December then again in late January, each drop in degree registered in your blood vessels.

§

"So, the cabinet thing makes you fight your worst fears?

"Yeah."

Ben insisted we watch Harry Potter because he learned I had stopped reading at book three. We were watching *The Prisoner of Azkaban* because he'd left off there in his re-viewing of the films. (I had too, I guess, just twenty years earlier.) In this scene, children were battling giant snakes and spiders that emerged from a magic armoire.

"I wonder what I'd fight," I said. "What does failure look like?"

He laughed and got up to smoke a cigarette in the biting December air. Gray smoke hovered outside, framed by the yellow-dark at the edges of his window.

I'd tried to explain my struggle with fantasy stories. It's not that I never liked Harry Potter; I'm too literally minded to get it. I'm too rooted in reality to extract myself from it.

"I just don't have a very good imagination."

"Well, there are different kinds of imagination."

"That's true," I said. I hadn't framed it that way before.

I always believed fantasy better suited those who wanted to flee to the outer edges of possibility and avoid reality. I imagined tangible careers and wealth and success growing up. I was living at the edge of a chaos cultivated by an alcoholic parent, and the only way I could imagine was to plan. I needed more than a metaphorical escape; what good would wishing for a broomstick have done for a girl whose only dream was to leave her family for real?

If we'd watched the Cabinet of Nightmares scene when I'd first met Ben, eight years earlier, I think my response would have been different. I'd moved from Montana to New York City at 18 to go to college. I pledged a sorority in my sophomore year and quit a few weeks in, realizing I had tried to find the same community I'd abandoned in high school at a college known for its high suicide rate and, like the city it resided in, was sometimes criticized for its solipsism. My disloyalty set the downfall of our pledge class in motion: two girls quit right after me. The three of us celebrated our re-found desire not to belong anywhere at one of their apartments, making crafts and getting drunk. Ben was my friend's live-in boyfriend at the time. He was nine years older than me, wore all black, and had a corporate job I didn't understand. He sat with my fellow pledge class dropouts and me while we glitter-glued cotton balls to construction paper. He poured us beer.

"From what I've heard, this sorority sounded really culty," he said.

"Yeah, I knew I had to leave as soon as they told me I couldn't leave," I said.

"I'm so glad you quit, Maryann," my former pledge sister confessed. "We wouldn't have quit if you didn't."

I lost touch with both sorority friends soon after we graduated. Five years after I met him—almost to the day—Ben and I started sleeping together.

§

Arizona winters are bland. The desert is dry and naked all year. Cacti retain their stoicism from month to month. The stars are unimpressive, like paint flecks on a tarp. No snow falls. It is endless beige. The weather doesn't allow for gray space.

§

My parents abandoned my home state as soon as I moved away. They didn't like the Montana winters. I was the last of four children to leave and the only one to never come back. I had nowhere to return to. They hadn't planned for me to go back to Bozeman, or visit them in Arizona, over any of my college winter breaks. The cost of flights and illogical logistics of the Northwest/Southwest/Northeast triangle made travel impractical.

After two months away at school, my parents asked if I wanted to visit them in Arizona for Christmas. I spent a snowless holiday in their retirement community where my gray-haired mother downed a bottle or two of wine each day and spent more of her time telling her friends how great I was than she did asking me how I was. I blended into the landscape, like one glittering sequin among hundreds on something from my mother's closet. No one would have noticed me missing.

A week later, my parents hugged me at the airport and sent me on a plane to Bozeman, where I would spend the week alone. My parents weren't worried I would throw wild parties, or starve, without supervision. They left me an empty house in Montana.

§

Montana winters are frigid and long. The snow-capped Rocky Mountain peaks loom above the suburban town of Bozeman all year, subtle reminders of the cold that will return. The summer landscape turns brown then white then gray. The days become overcast by cloud cover, but the night skies are vibrant with stars, their distant glimmers like reflections of snow in the atmosphere's mirrored black. Snow falls by mid-October and stays. It jackets the earth in infinite crystalline white. For a few days, before the SUVs and pick-up trucks have soiled it, the snow owns everything.

§

I was 19 my last winter visit to Montana. I'd met Ben a month before, the quintessential New Yorker: he wore all black; he smoked; he was nocturnal. My relationship with him then was that of an acquaintance, but I felt more anchored to the cold autonomy he projected—to New York—than I ever did to home. Growing up, I used to imagine the Rocky Mountains protecting me from what existed beyond them. When I returned that winter, I came to see them as jeering giants, reminding me how small I was. I didn't need a week in an empty house to know I didn't belong there either.

The night before I left, I saw my high school friends a final time. In the middle of the night, my former friends and I drove into a blizzard in search of whatever used to connect us. We landed at Wal-Mart. It was one of the few places open all night and large enough for a pack of teenagers to roam undetected through its aisles of snarky t-shirts, party-size packs of off-brand ice pops, children's toys, and guns—some just up for grabs on endcaps. We dispersed, each setting off on our own adventures through the empty aisles humming with fluorescence.

I awakened an aisle of Tickle-Me-Elmos, pressing each toy's belly and provoking it into laughter. Their adorable giggles amplified into a haunting reminder that, there, I was alone.

I also found an E-Z Bake Oven for $19.99. No sales tax.

I brought the piece of recovered childhood back to my house. My friends came with it. I got a bowl to mix the ingredients and found that a Dixie cup would have been more than sufficient. The packaged dust called for a teaspoon of water. E-Z Bake confections played to their audience: tiny hands with tiny stomachs. I loaded the cookie with the special handle. It was what had always appealed to me about the toy: it felt like a pizza oven. Although, a rudimentary understanding of science quickly kills the magic of a toy that cooks things with a 60-watt light bulb.

My friends huddled around the E-Z Bake, the yellow-dark fluttering at the edges of the sliding glass doors behind them. The nascent light of near-morning bounced off the immaculate snow sheath outside, untouched in our absence. My friends curled around the table—the table where I sat with my mother for an hour in a furniture store while the saleswoman explained how to play Spoons.

It was not the table of my childhood. Not the table where my sister showed me how to color. Not the table where my parents confronted Andromeda about her eating disorder. Not the table where we ate dinner as a family until I was 12. Not the table where our mother told us Arthur had a tumor removed from his shoulder.

My parents discarded my childhood with all the ease of a tattered t-shirt.

The table where Martin told me to test the hot glue by touching it, the table where I quit reading *Harry Potter*, the table scarred with wine stains and crayon marks and memories then served as a printer and computer prop cluttered with Mom's antique jewelry, spools of thread, and fabric scraps from her unfinished craft projects. It was the last camouflaged remnant of my childhood in that house. The rest had absconded, like my brothers and sister, or discarded before I hit eighth grade, when my parents and I moved across town.

I tried to hold on to my childhood through old friends, to take it back by buying a toy I'd never owned and marching it into an empty house. I've made it!

Look what I can do without you! But it was a familiar absence. The vaulted living room ceiling, the Montana mountain peaks, the missing mom and dad: their echoes dwarfed me. What resonated in Montana was its emptiness. My high school friends were friends of convenience and proximity in a vast landscape. We belonged because of where we lived, not who we were. Eventually, our divergent ambitions would set us on separate paths, and our imaginations could no longer sustain us on only the novelty of a children's toy.

Years later, the man I'd met a month before that last trip to Montana, in the icy cold of New York City, would remind me there is more than one kind of imagination, and that what you leave behind isn't always abandoned. My fantasies may have only reached as far as unrealized childhood baking dreams, but I had always seen a life for myself: one that was not defined by the geography I inhabited, but by my choice to live there. I had fantasized of a world where I could belong as an outlier, to be one glittering sequin amid snowflakes, landing on the slushy sidewalk and sticking, even just for a little while.

From the opposite end of the dining room table in my empty Montana house, I watched my then-friends smile and laugh, as if I were peering in from outside. I felt my snow-capped heart beating, beating, beating, and imagined its tiny reverberations off the plaster walls around me. I could feel it, desperate to get out. I was never afraid of solitude. I was afraid of being trapped.

The signature ding startled me lucid, beckoning us to our sugar cookie. I cut it into pieces, and it crumbled into powder. We ate it in seconds and left dry crumbs on the table.

§

Ben's cigarette smoke whispered into the black and floated up toward the few visible stars in Brooklyn. Soon, we too would fade like smoke in the night.

New York City winters sting. But at least you can feel them.

Little Astronaut

Marzipan passed away unexpectedly as I was completing this book. I came home on March 8th to find her wheezing on the floor, uninterested in her food. On March 9th, she died.

As soon as I got home that Wednesday, I Googled emergency vets, hoping something like that existed, and hurried to the pet hospital. There wasn't time to deal with her untouched food, or mine, as I scooped her and her racing heart up and out the door. When I arrived, the front desk nurses acted like she had a gunshot wound, calling over an intercom and rushing her to the backroom.

As patients named "Cleopatra" and "Zero" and "S'mores" came and went over the next four hours, I sat alone in the corner of the lobby, editing the thesis I had printed out that morning. I was two essays and a few dozen line edits away from finishing it. I'd left off reading earlier that day—just before "Satellites," an essay I'd thought was about moving furniture, but my graduate professor rightfully determined was about my cat.

I knew she wouldn't come home that night. I knew she might not come home ever.

But I hoped. I sat in that waiting room on the edge of conversion. I would have prayed to any god, called upon Odin and Ra and Zeus, to save her. There are no atheists in foxholes and there are no atheists in animal emergency rooms.

§

Two days earlier in my therapist's office, I was a clichéd depressive writer. *Oh! Woe is me…I have no future…I have nothing to keep me going.* Yet, I'd never tried to end my own life—I had only teetered at the precipice.

My therapist applauded my inner strength, something I deemed my "little astronaut." For years, I'd personified my depression; when it became unmanageable, I personified the other part of me—the one fighting against it. In that waiting room, I realized it was her tiny paws that got me out of bed each morning, the getting-dressed game in which she sat on whatever clothes I set on my bed, the gentle purrs of my bedmate that kept me going. She was a part of me. So much a part of me that I took her existence for granted. Marzipan was my brightest part. Like Orion's belt, she oriented me in my dark nights.

In Greek myth, when Orion the hunter was killed suddenly by a scorpion's sting, the goddesses asked Zeus to put him in the sky. The Orion constellation is one of the most colorful and recognizable in our universe. Orion's belt is made of three bright stars in an almost perfect straight line. The rest of the constellation forms the archer and his bow. The cluster contains the vivid Orion Nebula and two supergiants: Rigel and Betelgeuse, the 7th and 10th brightest stars in our universe.

§

In that waiting room, I felt my energy exhausted. I needed to keep going for her. I would have given her a kidney if we lived in a backwards world where cats and humans could trade organs. I would have spent $10,000 to save her. I would have signed 30 credit card agreements with 27 percent interest rates if not paid off in full in six months. (I have to wonder what kind of evil preys on desperate and lonely humans trying to save the only creatures they have loved so deeply.)

I went home at 2:00 a.m., Marzipan's diagnosis still unclear, except that she might not make it through the night. I said goodbye to her in a plastic oxygen chamber. She had a kitty catheter in her leg. I said goodbye then, trying to convince myself she would come home soon. Instead, she spent her last night in an unfamiliar hospital. She spent her last night without me.

When I came home, I opened the door and realized Marzipan wasn't there to greet me. She always knew when I was on my way, even if I was down the block. My roommates noted this, always impressed by my cat's very lame extrasensory abilities. And every day, she would be there when I opened the door.

That night I was alone. Unequivocally alone. For the first time in five years.

§

I took a $40 cab ride to work the next morning so I wouldn't miss a call from the vet. My coworkers told me to go home, but I couldn't stay there. I couldn't exist in a space without her. After so many years of bolstering my defenses against loss, I forgot about the one thing that lived inside my walls—I wasn't ready to let her go.

The critical specialist called me twenty minutes after I got to my office. I let myself believe she might have good news. She told me Marzipan had an infection. She wasn't responding to medication. Her chances of survival were less than 20 percent. The doctor said she could continue treating her—it could be cancer, she said, though most likely not—and she suggested I euthanize Marzipan. Though I lack faith in a god of any kind, I believe in science. And I believe in the limitations of it.

I had always told myself I wouldn't make her live in pain.

"Well, because of the medication she is on, I don't think she's in pain right now" the vet told me. "She's woozy, maybe. But not in pain."

I was crying. My tear ducts were like faulty spigots, spurting water at random whether or not I turned them on. "I have an interview today…" I said into the ether. "Can you— is there… can you make her comfortable until six?"

"I'm not sure she'll make it until six."

I felt horrible for even asking. How could I have even considered waiting? What kind of heartless beast was I? The makeup I'd put on for my interview washed down my face like the rusty brown from a broken faucet. I stood up and shoved an unprocessed invoice on my supervisor's desk, speaking in half-sentences.

"I have to go. I have to— to— I'm sorry. I have to go put my cat down…I can't." I flailed my hand at the invoice.

My coworker and supervisor walked me down to the lobby. I climbed into the backseat of a Lyft and blurted that I was going to put my cat down. My crying was acting of its own volition, and I knew it wouldn't stop; I felt I owed this stranger an explanation. The driver dug through his glove compartment for some napkins to offer me.

"I'm sorry I don't have any tissues," he said, "but you can use these if you want."

At the front desk of the animal clinic, I said I was there for Marzipan.

"You can come right back," the nurse told me.

They brought her in to me, wrapped in a blanket covered in stars and moons. They told me I could have as long as I wanted.

She was frail and afraid, clear tubes radiating from her body. There was a tiny yellow one stitched near her nose. When they handed her to me, I felt like I had been split open.

"I didn't know she was so sick," I said. The doctor reassured me that cats are adept at hiding their illnesses; we often can't tell they're sick until it's too late. All I could think was how depressed I'd been in the past few months; how much I'd struggled to keep myself alive. The vet said she didn't think it would have made a difference had I brought her in two months or a week or a day earlier. It wasn't my fault.

"It was acute. She deteriorated rapidly. You should take comfort knowing you did everything you could."

Holding her frail and septic body, I felt so horrifically guilty. And so horrifically sad. I tried to adjust her in my lap *just the way you like it, princess.* She wheezed and I waited, thinking she might go then. *Hoping* she might pass right then. Hoping I might go with her, the two of us evaporating in a stark hospital room.

But something lit within her. She lifted her head and writhed. I wanted to let her sit up, to be wild, but she wriggled away from me, her back leg was wrapped with tape to hold the intravenous tube pumping kitty drugs into her system, keeping her barely alive—for me. She fell into a pile of herself on the floor. I heaved in sobs, jumping to the floor to get to her—I had been unbuttoned. All my insides spilled out as I leaned over, a pile of myself, to scoop her up. I'd tried to hold on to her too long. I knew she would fight for hours, wheezing and flinging herself to the floor. But I had to let her take flight.

I rested her on my seat so I could run to the door and find someone. A nurse passed by, and I squeezed out commands between sobs.

"Please. Can you get someone? She's…I want to do it now."

The nurse sprinted to the back room, and I ran to Marzipan, angry at myself for leaving her alone on a chair for even a moment. I lifted her as gently as I could and realized my hand was wet. She peed, unable to control her own body anymore, but I held my hand there. I held it as if to tell her it was ok. She could pee wherever she wanted. She could pee all over the world that did this to her. I wouldn't let go of her.

I told her she was a brave girl and, even as her urine splashed onto my only-worn-once-but-still-covered-in-cat-hair pants, I held her and whispered *I'm sorry. I'm so sorry. I love you so much. My brave girl.*

The nurse returned, flanked by the doctor and a receptionist. One of them shoved a clipboard in my hand and the other cupped Marzipan in her hands so I could sign. I had to give permission to euthanize her and choose what I wanted to do with her remains.

I wanted her ashes. I never thought I would be the person who owned her cat's ashes, but at the time, anything else felt absolutely absurd. *Of course*, I wanted her ashes.

The doctor had asked me earlier if I wanted to be present.

"Absolutely," I said. I couldn't let her die anywhere but in my arms.

The vet explained the series of drugs she would administer, the final being an overdose of anesthesia. I took a crumb of comfort in knowing she'd be done in by sleep—her favorite activity. I held her and stroked her and told her I loved her. I told her I was sorry this was happening, and she was so brave, and I loved her. I told her I loved her, as if she could understand me. Because I didn't know if the turkey slices I'd fed her the week before were enough. Because I didn't know if the Ben & Jerry's ice cream lid I'd let her lick (all right, I gave her a little extra—she liked ice cream) two days earlier was enough. Because I didn't know if my own warm body heat against hers every night was enough. Because I read a line in this book where I questioned all that and, while I could edit it away, truth is inconstant. It was true when I wrote it and will always have been true. Now, the truth is different.

"Her heart has stopped," the doctor said. My hand kept stroking her still-warm head.

I envy my cat for being able to exist in silence. I held her briefly, in permanent slumber.

"Would you like more time with her?"

"I don't know," I said, still petting her.

I'd wanted to go back in time. To find a black hole and dive into it and find out if Einstein was right. To take a leap of faith in my god, Science. I wanted to rescue her all over again—I'd adopted her five and half years earlier from the ASPCA. She used to hunt mice in my first apartment. She left one on my bed once. I also found one dead in her water dish. I was always a little bit proud of that. She did the same thing with a cockroach. Sometimes, she would bring me a toy mouse and leave it in my bed. We went through four or five of them as each one deteriorated from saliva and claw marks. She was a hunter, always protecting me from the vermin of the world.

I thought I'd have another five years with her. But I came home one night, and she was gone the next. The vet assured me it wasn't my fault. It was biology. Sepsis brought on by an acute gallbladder infection.

I'd done everything I could have—$1900 worth of could have. But, of course, I felt guilty. Of course, I remembered every night I came home late or didn't spend with her. Or course I thought about the times I fed her breakfast an hour late. Of course, I worried that I didn't love her enough when she was alive—or that she didn't know it. I took her for granted because she was a part of me. The brightest part.

Marzipan came to me on a sunny March day wrapped in stars, ready to say goodbye. The next morning, it snowed for her. The sky froze and cried for her. And my heart splintered. I have never loved anything so much.

As I embrace the crazy person I've become—already planning what kind of tattoo I can get to memorialize her, researching how to put cat ashes in glass orbs, and fantasizing about driving around with an urn of her in the front seat (she would have finally conquered her fear of the car)—I realize I may have been wrong about soulmates. I think I found mine in a cat who loved cold cuts and hated other cats.

Outside, when it is dark, and visible through the space between my curtains is a single star, I will think of Marzipan. I'll imagine her sparkling in the night sky, pawing at my chin for food, or nestled on my chest, comforting us both.

I will think of Orion and all the bright stars Zeus placed in him. I'll think of the supergiant Betelgeuse, a star 500 times the size of the sun. If it were placed at the center of our solar system, it would engulf Mercury, Venus, Earth, Mars, and Jupiter. In the instant when it explodes, Betelgeuse will release more energy into the universe than our sun will in its lifetime.

Until then, I will continue my orbit, knowing she is my little astronaut— my piece of strength—now returned to the sky to be painted in stars. There, she can sleep in her perfect gray circle, undisturbed among one hundred octillion stars.

Appendix

An earlier version of this book contained 16 essays, each titled with the name of a constellation, a description, and image. This didn't suit the final version, but it was important to cultivating the collection. The original constellation titles are presented here, in the order they originally appeared. I've also noted which essays they correspond to. North Star was the 17th essay added to the collection and never had a constellation title.

Sextans, The Sextant
(Orbit)

Sextans is a constellation named for the sextant; an 18ᵗʰ-century instrument used for naval navigation. Sextants measure angles between celestial objects and the horizon. Sextans rests in a dim and sparse area of the sky where the moon, and sometimes planets, pass through it.

Horologium, The Pendulum Clock

(Dawn)

The constellation Horologium, or pendulum clock, is a dim constellation in the southern sky. Pendulum clocks rely on a swinging weight to keep time. Because the weight sways back and forth at a consistent rate, these clocks keep precise time as long as they remain still. Motion can disrupt the rate at which the pendulum swings, causing inaccuracies.

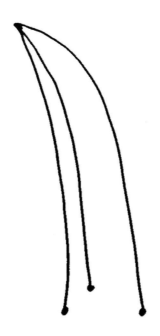

Cepheus, The King of Aethiopia
(Porn Star)

Cepheus, named after Cassiopeia's husband, is a bright constellation in the northern sky. It contains some of the largest known stars—an orange hypergiant and several red supergiants—and quasar S5 0014+81, which is home to the largest black hole in the known universe. Cepheus was the father of Andromeda.

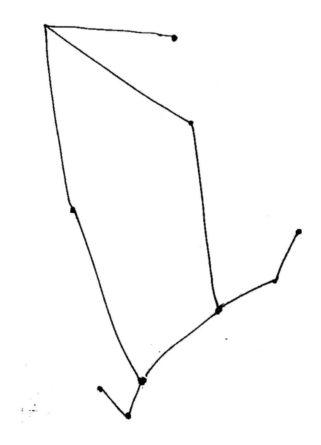

Cassiopeia, The Vain Queen

(Supernova)

Cassiopeia sits opposite the Big Dipper in the northern sky. It's easily visible because of the five bright stars making up its distinctive "W" shape. The constellation contains remnants of a supernova. It's named for Cassiopeia, the vain queen in Greek mythology who often bragged about her own beauty as well as her daughter's. Because of her bragging, Cassiopeia sacrificed her daughter, Andromeda, to save her and Cepheus's kingdom.

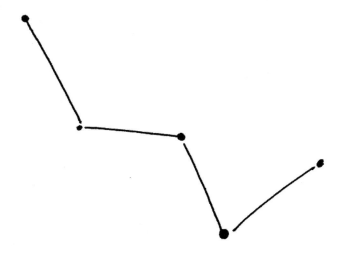

Sculptor

(Vanishing Star/North Star*)

Sculptor is a small and faint constellation in the La Caille family. This family of constellations consists of a dozen formations made of faint stars that were likely invisible to the Greeks and Romans. In the late 18ᵗʰ century, Nicolas Louis de La Caille discovered the Sculptor with a telescope. Originally, he named it Apparatus Sculptoris, "the sculptor's studio."

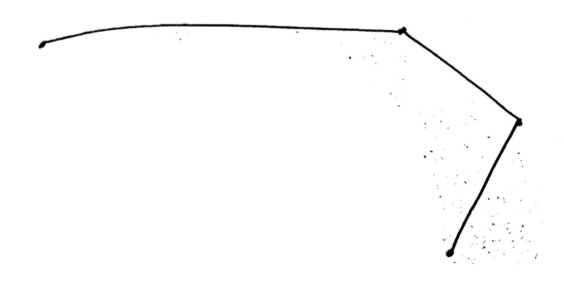

**This essay ended up being split into two essays,
Vanishing Star and North Star.*

Leo Minor, The Little Lion

(Satellites)

Leo minor is a faint constellation representing a lion cub. It was established by Johannes Hevelius in 1687, so it was not known to the ancient Greeks. Because of its position between the large and prominent Leo and Ursa Major, Leo Minor is often missed in the night sky. Though small, it contains the orange giant Leonis Minoris and a rare celestial object: Hanny's Voorwerp, a gas cloud the size of a galaxy.

Andromeda, The Chained Princess

(The Geography of Flight)

Andromeda is brightest in autumn; it lies in the northern hemisphere. It is one of the largest constellations and home to the radiant of the Andromedids meteor shower. The constellation is named after the princess Andromeda whose parents—Cassiopeia and Cepheus—chained her to a rock to be eaten by Cetus, the sea monster.

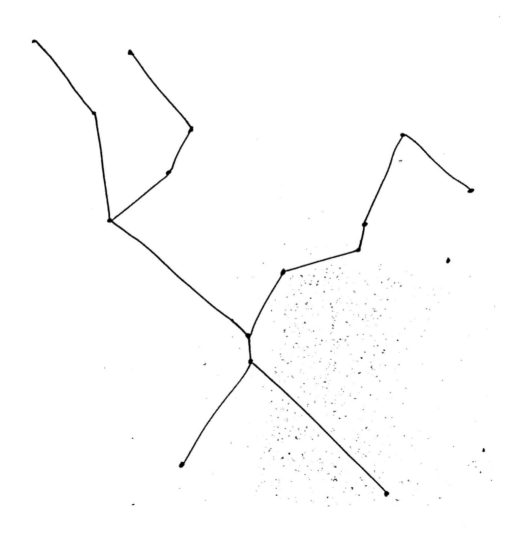

Eridanus, The River
(Quiet)

Eridanus is often represented as a river, but it is also connected to the myth of Phaethon. Eridanus is the path Phaethon took when Zeus struck him to earth after losing control of Helios's chariot. It is the sixth-largest constellation and one of the original 48 Greek constellations discovered by Ptolemy. Several modern rivers are named after the constellation.

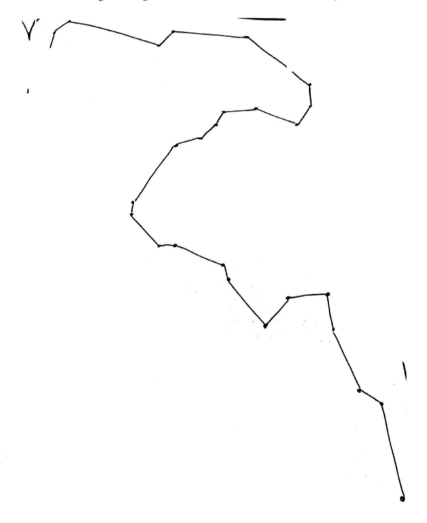

Ursa Major/Ursa Minor: A One-Woman Show

(Star Child: A One-Woman Show)

Ursa Major is the Great Bear; it contains the "Big Dipper." It is the third largest constellation in the sky and one of the most well-known constellations throughout history.

Ursa Minor is the Little Bear or the "Little Dipper." It marks the north celestial pole. Ursa Minor's handle is home to Polaris, the North Star, which was often used to guide sailors and travelers.

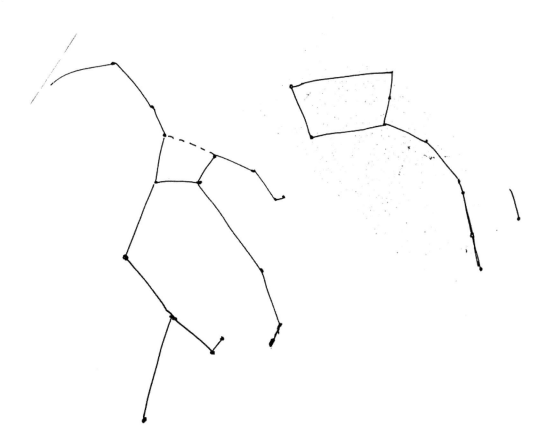

Perseus, The Hero

(Stellar Remnants)

Perseus is a constellation in the northern sky. Part of the Milky Way passes through the constellation, which contains the radiant of the prominent Perseids meteor shower.

It is named for the Greek hero who, by coincidence, found Andromeda chained to a rock and slayed Cetus, the sea monster she was sacrificed to. He rescued the princess and the two married.

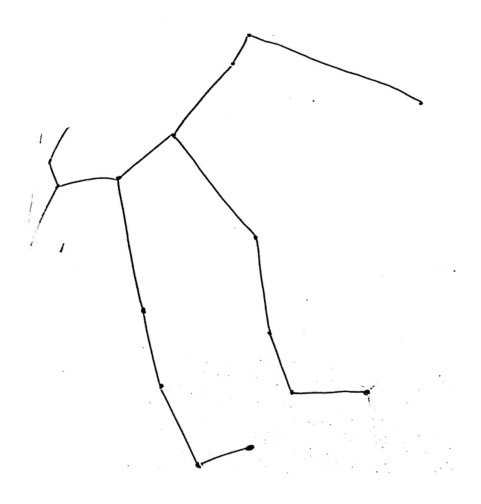

Virgo, The Virgin

(Virginity Limbo)

Virgo is the largest Zodiac constellation and the second largest of all 88 modern constellations. The Virgo Cluster is a group of galaxies closest to our own. The cluster is so large, it spills into the adjacent constellations. Virgo also contains the brightest Quasar, 3C 273. In Greek mythology, Virgo took on the identities of both Demeter, goddess of the harvest and fertility, and Dike, the goddess of justice.

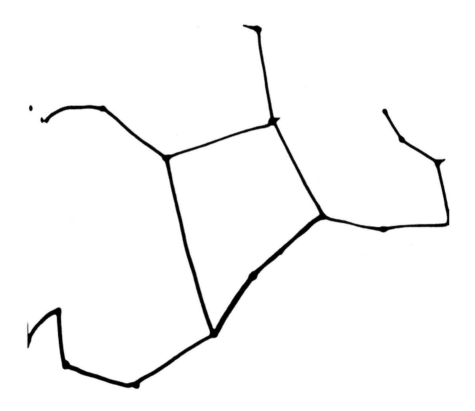

Cetus, The Sea Monster

(Leviathan)

Cetus is the fourth largest of the modern constellations. It's found in a part of the sky called the Water. Cetus is named for the sea monster unleashed by Poseidon after the queen Cassiopeia bragged that her daughter, Andromeda, was more beautiful than the Nereids. Angered by her boastfulness, Poseidon set Cetus on Cepheus and Cassiopeia's kingdom. To save their people, they chained Andromeda to a rock as a sacrifice to the monster. Perseus, who walked by at just the right moment, slayed Cetus with Medusa's head and rescued Andromeda, freeing her from her chains.

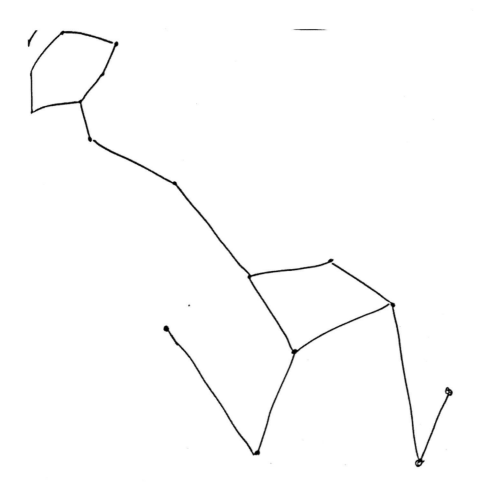

Apus, The Exotic Bird

(Lunar Bodies)

Apus is a small constellation made of four bright stars. It is named for the bird-of-paradise and translates to "without feet." It was once believed that the bird-of-paradise had no feet. The Milky Way covers most of the constellation.

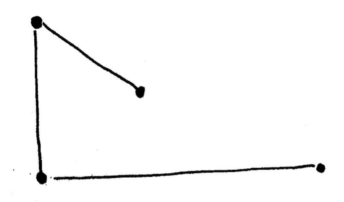

Chamaeleon, The Chameleon

(Neon Disguises)

Chamaeleon is a constellation in the southern sky; its brightest star is Alpha Chamaeleontis. It contains a planetary nebula, the Chamaeleon cloud complex, and the Eta Chamaeleontis Cluster. The constellation is named for the chameleon, a lizard able to camouflage itself by changing colors. Their pigmented skin cells allow chameleons to change color rapidly and blend in to almost any background—artificial or not.

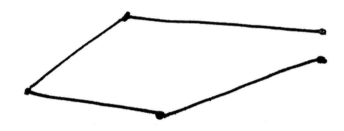

Triangulum, The Triangle
(Dusk)

The triangle constellation was originally conceived as the Greek letter Delta, but eventually became a simple isosceles triangle. Made of three bright stars, Triangulum is bordered by Andromeda and Perseus.

Orion, The Hunter

(Little Astronaut)

The constellation Orion is named after the great hunter Orion in Greek mythology. He was killed suddenly by a scorpion's sting, and after his death, the goddesses asked Zeus to put Orion in the sky. Though it is best visible in winter, from December through February, Orion is widely recognized by stargazers. Many locate the eternal portrait by finding Orion's Belt, an almost straight line of three bright stars: Alnitak, Alnilam, and Mintaka. It is one of the brightest and most colorful constellations because it contains the vivid Orion Nebula, the red supergiant Betelgeuse, and the blue supergiant Rigel—the 7th brightest star in the sky. Betelgeuse, which rests on the hunter's shoulder, is 500 times the size of the sun. If it were placed at the center of our solar system, it would engulf Mercury, Venus, Earth, Mars, and Jupiter. In the instant when it explodes, Betelgeuse will release more energy into the universe than our sun will in its lifetime.

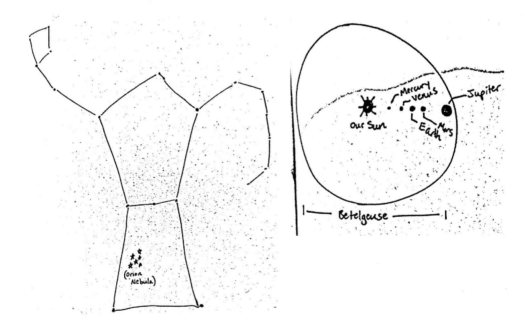

Acknowledgements

I'm grateful to the following journals for taking on a chance on these essays: "Vanishing Star" appeared in *The Porter House Review.* "The Geography of Flight" was first published in *Big Muddy: A Journal of the Mississippi River Valley* and reprinted in *The Coachella Review.* "Stellar Remnants," originally titled "Artifacts," appeared in *The Exposition Review,* as did "Lunar Bodies." *Crack the Spine* first published "Neon Disguises," which was later reprinted in *Eunoia Review.* "Dusk" appeared in *perhappened magazine* as "Frostbite." "Quiet" references "On the Phenomenon of Sudden Death in Animals and Man," a 1957 study published by Curt Richter, Ph.D. in *Psychosomatic Medicine,* Volume 19, Issue 3.

This book would have not been possible if not for the emotional and intellectual support of many people, some of who I will probably forget to thank due to the stress-induced amnesia that is publishing a book. Little Astronaut would be no more than an unruly Word document on my computer if not for Ariana Den Bleyker, who I will never be able to thank profusely enough for believing in this strange little book and giving it a loving home. I'm also especially grateful for her work on the incredibly tedious layout required to fulfill my vision of experimental literature. Who else would print an unknown author's debut essay collection in 7x 9 format? Thank you, thank you, thank you.

Thanks to you, Reader, for picking it up and flipping to the acknowledgements page to see if your name is in it (it is! kind of). I hope you bought it from a local bookstore and if you didn't, I hope you stole it from an enemy.

An enormous thank you to Jo Ann Beard for being the first champion of this book, in its earliest form, when she was my MFA thesis advisor. I am forever humbled to have had her support. Thank you, Jo Ann, for your astute criticism and unbridled enthusiasm.

I also want to thank the entire Sarah Lawrence College MFA program and Brian Morton, Paige Ackerson-Kiely, and Amparo Rios for running it, as well as my professors and colleagues who encouraged, challenged, and inspired me, and made my work better. Thank you to Jacob Slichter (for his guidance and stellar cover blurb), Fred Strype, Tiphanie Yanique, Monica Youn, Tim Kreider,

D. Nurkse, and Suzanne Hoover for helping shape this book and sharpen my voice. Many thanks are due to my entire cohort for their energy and creativity, especially to those who read early drafts of these essays: Christine, (who I also owe for the book title inspiration), Cathy, Jordan, Rachel P., Rachel A., and Ally Sofer, who I am very sad will never get to read this book nor will the world get to read hers.

Thanks to David Wojciechowski for his incredible cover design and Kira Sutherland for the beautiful book-inspired artwork I have been using in marketing materials.

Thank you to Kristine Langley Mahler for an encouraging rejection and an even more encouraging first blurb for this book. I cannot express what a relief it was to know my book's back cover would not be naked.

To the writers I looked to when crafting this book (that I haven't already mentioned), who all treated me with the utmost generosity when the time came for the dreaded asking for blurbs: Paul Lisicky (who allowed me to use his words on the front *and* back cover!), Kelly Sundberg, Jessamyn Hope, and Melissa Febos.

Thanks to Emily Flake for the St. Nell's Humor Writing Residency for Ladies, where I did very little work on this book, though the time and space there was invaluable to its conclusion, nonetheless. To Mai and Sandi for our writing "research" and the town of Williamsport for their YMCA where I got my ass in shape again so that I could perhaps endure a book tour.

I am grateful to Barrelhouse Writer Camp simply for existing, but also for giving me the break I needed (and copious amounts of bug spray) to revise the manuscript into what it is now. Most of all, though, I owe Writer Camp for giving me the courage to fail at beer pong in my 30s. A special thank you to our makeshift nonfiction workshop, Stephanie, Harmony, and Steve, for their remarkable words (and for their leap of faith in my competency as a writer). Bonus points to Steve for his shockingly astute interviewing skills, which helped me figure out that the essay "Porn Star" was what was missing from the collection.

Thanks to Emily Schleiger for my first official author interview in *The Coachella Review,* and to all the journals who have championed my words and to all those who will. Thanks to the presses who declined this manuscript with kind words that kept me going. Thanks to the Binders and Carla Starrett-Bigg and Gabrielle Kaplan-Mayer for loving "Vanishing Star" so much they agreed to read the entire book and say nice things about it.

Thanks to my OSF colleagues who are the first coworkers I truly considered friends, who, for some reason, seem to like learning about my deepest childhood traumas.

Thanks to "Ben," even though it wasn't written in the stars for us, for never asking me to change my story.

To my former therapist, Molly, who plays only a small explicit role in these pages, but whose support made many of these pieces come to fruition. She helped me find my little astronaut, even in the times I was
most worried I would drown.

To my psychiatrist, Dr. Neushotz, who is much of the reason I am still here to publish this book.

To all the cats I have loved, currently love, and will ever love.

Without the support of my friends, I probably wouldn't even tell people about this book. Thanks especially to Amanda, Elyse, VJ, Ali, Joanna, Jordan, Hannah, Jared, Greg, Alex, Dominic, Chloe, and Natassja for believing in me, always, and thanks to all the friends who have ever rescued me. Thanks to Erensu for being my roommate, confidante, friend, fake publicist, real lawyer, and tasting-menu adventurer. But also, thank you for seeing a copy of my thesis and asking to read it, unprompted. It meant the world to me.

A special thank you to my parents, who may never know this book exists, but gave me the ability to write it.

To my siblings, I love you all more than I can convey in even 40,000 words. Thank you most of all to my sister, for giving me this story and the strength to tell it. You all deserve to be drawn in the stars someday.

About the Author

Maryann Aita (ATE-uh) is a writer and performer in Brooklyn, New York. Her work has appeared in *PANK Magazine*, which earned a Best of the Net nomination, *The Porter House Review*, *perhappened mag*, *The Daily Drunk, The Exposition Review*, and other journals. She is also the nonfiction editor of *Press Pause Press*. Maryann is a St. Nell's Humor Residency for Ladies Fellow, and she performs around New York City, including her one-woman-show *My Dysfunctional Vagina*. She has an MFA in writing from Sarah Lawrence College and lives with three cats. Follow her on Twitter and Instagram @maryann_aita